Includes Yellowstone & Grand Teton National Parks

Birds of Wyoming

Field Guide
by Stan Tekiela

Adventure Publications
Cambridge, Minnesota

To Dan and Alyssa Tekiela, enjoy Wyoming.

Acknowledgments

Many thanks to the National Wildlife Refuge System along with state and local agencies, both public and private, for stewarding lands that are critical to the many bird species we so love.

Edited by Sandy Livoti

Book design and illustrations by Jonathan Norberg

Range maps produced by Anthony Hertzel

Photo credits by photographer and page number:

Cover photo: Western Tanager by Stan Tekiela
Paul Bannick: 330 (non-breeding male) **Rick and Nora Bowers**: 52 (non-breeding male), 110, 126, 136, 204 (all), 258 (winter), 282, 292, 294, 306 (winter, juvenile), 314 (female), 330 (female), 332 **Dudley Edmondson**: 258 (breeding) **Kevin T. Karlson**: 54 (male inset), 216 (female) **Maslowski Wildlife Productions**: 90 (female) **Brian E. Small**: 118 (female) **Jacob S. Spendelow**: 230 (Audubon's female) **Stan Tekiela**: 22, 24, 26 (both), 28, 30, 32, 34, 36 (both), 38, 40, 42 (both), 44 (both), 46 (perching, soaring), 48 (all), 50 (both), 52 (male), 54 (both winter), 56 (both), 58 (both), 60 (both), 62 (winter), 64, 66, 68, 70 (both), 72, 74, 76 (displaying male, non-displaying), 78 (all), 80 (both), 82 (all), 84, 86, 88, 90 (male), 92 (both), 96, 98 (both), 100, 102, 104, 106, 108 (female, pink-sided), 112, 114, 116 (both), 118 (male), 120 (female), 122, 124 (both), 128, 130, 132 (all), 134 (both), 138, 140, 142 (all), 144, 146, 148 (both), 150 (both), 152, 154 (all), 156, 158 (both), 160, 162 (all), 164 (both), 166 (both), 168 (both), 170, 172, 174 (perching, both flight), 176 (both), 178 (both), 180, 182, 184, 186, 188, 190, 192 (both), 194, 196 (soaring), 198 (all), 200 (both light morphs), 202 (Western soaring, both Eastern), 206, 208 (perching, both soaring), 210 (both), 212 (perching, soaring), 214 (all), 216 (male, both insets), 218, 220 (both), 222, 224, 226 (male, Oregon male), 228 (both), 230 (Audubon's male, all Myrtle), 232, 234, 236, 238, 240, 242, 244 (both), 246 (both), 248, 250 (soaring, juvenile), 252, 254, 256, 258 (in flight), 260 (perching, soaring), 262 (male, female), 264 (displaying male, non-displaying), 266, 268 (both), 270 (all), 272 (both), 274 (both), 276 (both), 278 (both), 280, 284, 286, 288 (male, in flight), 290, 296 (male, yellow male), 298, 300, 302, 304 (female, in flight), 306 (breeding, in flight), 308 (all), 310 (all), 312 (all), 314 (male), 316 (all), 318 (male), 320, 322, 324 (both), 326, 328, 330 (male), 334 (all), 336, 338 **Brian K. Wheeler**: 46 (juvenile), 148 (both juveniles), 196 (female), 200 (both dark morphs, intermediate morph), 202 (Western perching), 208 (juvenile perching), 212 (both juveniles), 260 (juvenile) **Jim Zipp**: 62 (breeding), 76 (female), 94, 108 (Oregon female), 148 (in flight), 174 (juvenile), 250 (perching), 318 (female)

To the best of the publisher's knowledge, all photos were of live birds. Some were photographed in a controlled condition.

10 9 8 7 6 5 4 3
Birds of Wyoming Field Guide
Copyright © 2017 by Stan Tekiela
Published by Adventure Publications, an imprint of AdventureKEEN
310 Garfield Street South, Cambridge, Minnesota 55008
(800) 678-7006
www.adventurepublications.net
All rights reserved
Printed in China
ISBN 978-1-59193-725-8 (pbk.); ISBN: 978-1-59193-726-5 (ebook)

TABLE OF CONTENTS

WHY WATCH BIRDS IN WYOMING?

Millions of people have discovered bird feeding. It's a simple and enjoyable way to bring the beauty of birds closer to your home. Watching birds at your feeder and listening to them sing their songs often leads to a lifetime pursuit of bird identification. The *Birds of Wyoming Field Guide* is for those who want to identify the common birds found in Wyoming, including the Yellowstone and Grand Teton National Parks.

There are over 1,100 species of birds found in North America. In Wyoming alone there have been over 400 different kinds of birds recorded throughout the years. This is an impressive number of species for one state! These bird sightings were diligently recorded by hundreds of bird watchers and became part of the official state record. From these valuable records, I've chosen 134 of the most common and easily seen birds of Wyoming to include in this book.

Bird watching, or birding, is one of the most popular activities in America. Its appeal throughout Wyoming is due, in part, to an unusually rich and abundant birdlife. Why are so many birds in the state? The main reasons are open space and wide range of habitats. Wyoming covers around 97,800 square miles (253,300 sq. km). This is an exceedingly large area that includes most of Yellowstone and all of Grand Teton National Parks, which help make Wyoming a remarkable place to see a variety of birds.

Wyoming is one of the top ten largest states in the nation, with a total population of just over a half-million people. This averages to fewer than 6 people per square mile (2 per sq. km), making it the second-least densely populated state. Most of its residents live in four major cities scattered around the state.

Besides open space, Wyoming has several distinct habitats–mountain ranges, foothills and the High Plains–each of which supports a different group of birds.

In northwest Wyoming, mountains make up a quarter of the state and include the Absaroka, Wind River and Wyoming Ranges. These mountains are home to birds such as Mountain Bluebirds and American Dippers.

The foothills lead up the higher mountain peaks and have their own unique set of birds. Usually the habitat is a combination of open meadows and woodlands. Here you'll see birds such as Calliope Hummingbirds and Western Tanagers.

The High Plains are in the eastern two-thirds of the state. This area is generally flat or gently rolling topography. It is a diverse area, with the Bighorn, Sweetwater and North Platte Rivers making up much of its features. Wyoming's High Plains are home to birds such as Lazuli Buntings and Spotted Towhees.

Wyoming also has millions of acres of national forestland and, of course, two of the most popular national parks in the United States. In fact, the U.S. government owns more than 48 percent of the state in parks, refuges and BLM land. Many birds, such as Lark Buntings, Western Meadowlarks and Black-billed Magpies, are attracted to these open regions.

The weather also varies in Wyoming. The western mountains create a moisture barrier that results in a rain shadow effect in eastern Wyoming, making it much drier and windier there. Winters have periods of extreme cold interspersed by mild stretches. Summers can be very warm and much windier than in many other regions of the country, but in higher elevations, summers can be quite pleasant and moist.

From the mountains and rivers to the High Plains and majestic Yellowstone and Grand Teton National Parks, Wyoming is one of the best places in North America to watch an assortment of birds. Whether you're seeing Trumpeter Swans in Yellowstone or welcoming back hummingbirds to your yard during spring, there's variety and excitement in birding as each season turns to the next.

OBSERVE WITH A STRATEGY;
TIPS FOR IDENTIFYING BIRDS

Identifying birds isn't as difficult as you might think. By simply following a few basic strategies, you can increase your chances of successfully identifying most birds you see! One of the first and easiest things to do when you see a new bird is to note its color. (Also, since this book is organized by color, you will go right to that color section to find it.)

Next, note the size of the bird. A strategy to quickly estimate size is to select a small-, medium- and large-sized bird to use for reference. For example, most people are familiar with robins. A robin, measured from tip of the bill to tip of the tail, is 10 inches (25 cm) long. Using the robin as an example of a medium-sized bird, select two other birds, one smaller and one larger. Many people use a House Sparrow, at about 6 inches (15 cm), and an American Crow, about 18 inches (45 cm). When you see a bird that you don't know, you can quickly ask yourself, "Is it smaller than a robin, but larger than a sparrow?" When you look in your field guide to help identify your bird, you'll know it is roughly between 6-10 inches (15-25 cm) long. This will help to narrow your choices.

Next, note the size, shape and color of the bill. Is it long, short, thick, thin, pointed, blunt, curved or straight? Seed-eating birds, such as Evening Grosbeaks, have bills that are thick and strong enough to crack even the toughest seeds. Birds that sip nectar, such as Broad-tailed Hummingbirds, need long thin bills to reach deep into flowers. Hawks and owls tear their prey with very sharp, curving bills. Sometimes, just noting the bill shape can help you decide whether the bird is a woodpecker, sparrow, grosbeak, blackbird or bird of prey.

Next, take a look around and note the habitat in which you see the bird. Is it wading in a marsh? Walking along a riverbank? Soaring in the sky? Is it perched high in the trees or hopping along the forest floor? Because of their preferences in diet and habitat, you will usually see robins hopping on the ground, but not often eating seeds at a feeder. Or you'll see a Black-headed Grosbeak sitting on a tree branch, but not climbing headfirst down a tree trunk like a White-breasted Nuthatch.

Noticing what a bird is eating will give you another clue to help you identify that bird. Feeding is a big part of any bird's life. Fully one-third of all bird activity revolves around searching for and catching food, or actually eating. While birds don't always follow all the rules of what we think they eat, you can make some general assumptions. Northern Flickers, for instance, feed upon ants and other insects, so you wouldn't expect to see them visiting a backyard feeder. Some birds, such as Barn Swallows and Tree Swallows, feed upon flying insects and spend hours swooping and diving to catch a meal.

Sometimes you can identify a bird by the way it perches. Body posture can help you differentiate between an American Crow and a Red-tailed Hawk. American Crows lean forward over their feet on a branch, while hawks perch in a vertical position. Look for this the next time you see a large unidentified bird in a tree.

Birds in flight are often difficult to identify, but noting the size and shape of the wing will help. A bird's wing size is in direct proportion to its body size, weight and type of flying. The shape of the wing determines if the bird flies fast and with precision, or slowly and less precisely. Birds such as House Finches, which flit around in thick tangles of branches, have short, round wings. Birds that soar on warm updrafts of air, such as Turkey Vultures, have long, broad wings. Barn Swallows have short, pointed wings that slice through the air, propelling their swift and accurate flight.

Some birds have unique patterns of flight that aid in identification. American Goldfinches fly in a distinctive up-and-down pattern that makes it look as if they are riding a roller coaster.

While it's not easy to make these observations in the short time you often have to watch a "mystery bird," practicing these methods of identification will greatly expand your skills in birding. Also, seek the guidance of a more experienced birder who will help you improve your skills and answer questions on the spot.

BIRD BASICS

It's easier to identify birds and communicate about them if you know the names of the different parts of a bird. For instance, it's more effective to use the word "crest" to indicate the set of extra-long feathers on top of the head of a Steller's Jay than to try to describe it.

The following illustration points out the basic parts of a bird. Because it's a composite of many birds, it shouldn't be confused with any actual bird.

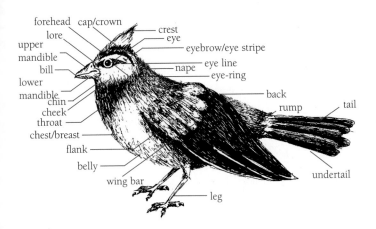

Bird Color Variables

No other animal has a color palette like a bird's. Brilliant blues, lemon yellows, showy reds and iridescent greens are commonplace within the bird world. In general, the male birds are more colorful than their female counterparts. This is probably to help the male attract a mate, essentially saying, "Hey, look at me!" It also calls attention to the male's overall health. The better the condition of his feathers, the better his food source and territory, and therefore the better his potential for a mate.

Female birds that don't look like their male counterparts (such species are called sexually dimorphic, meaning "two forms") are often a nondescript color, as seen in Lazuli Buntings. These muted tones help hide the females during weeks of motionless incubation, and draw less attention to them when they are out feeding or taking a break from the rigors of raising their young.

In some species, such as the Bald Eagle, Steller's Jay and Downy Woodpecker, male birds look nearly identical to the females. In the case of woodpeckers, the sexes are differentiated by only a single red mark or sometimes a yellow mark. Depending upon the species, the mark may be on top of the head, face, nape of neck or just behind the bill.

During the first year, juvenile birds often look like the mothers. Since brightly colored feathers are used mainly for attracting a mate, young non-breeding males don't have a need for colorful plumage. It is not until the first spring molt (or several years later, depending on the species) that young males obtain their breeding colors.

Both breeding and winter plumages are the result of molting. Molting is the process of dropping old worn feathers and replacing them with new ones. All birds molt, typically twice a year, with the spring molt usually occurring in late winter. During this time, most birds produce their breeding plumage (brighter colors for attracting mates), which lasts throughout the summer.

Winter plumage is the result of the late summer molt, which serves a couple of important functions. First, it adds feathers for warmth in the coming winter season. Second, in some species it produces feathers that tend to be drab in color, which helps to camouflage the birds and hide them from predators.

The winter plumage of the male American Goldfinch, for example, is olive brown unlike its obvious canary yellow color during summer. Luckily for us, some birds, such as Lewis's Woodpeckers, retain their bright summer colors all year long.

Bird Nests

Bird nests are truly an amazing feat of engineering. Imagine building your home strong enough to weather a storm, large enough to hold your entire family, insulated enough to shelter them from cold and heat, and waterproof enough to keep out rain. Now, build it without any blueprints or directions, and without the use of your hands or feet! Birds do!

Before building a nest, an appropriate site must be selected. In some species, such as House Wrens, the male picks out several potential sites and assembles several small twigs in each. This discourages other birds from using nearby nest cavities. These "extra" nests are occasionally called dummy nests. The female is then taken around and shown all the choices. She chooses her favorite and finishes constructing the nest. In some other species of birds–Bullock's Orioles, for example–it is the female who chooses the site and constructs the nest, with the male offering only an occasional suggestion. Each species has its own nest-building routine, which is strictly followed.

As you'll see in the following illustrations, birds build a wide variety of nest types.

| **ground nest** | **platform nest** | **cup nest** | **pendulous nest** | **cavity nest** |

Nesting material often consists of natural elements found in the immediate area. Most nests consist of plant fibers (such as bark peeled from grapevines), sticks, mud, dried grass, feathers, fur, or soft fuzzy tufts from thistle. Some birds, including Broad-tailed Hummingbirds, use spider webs to glue nest materials together. Nesting material is limited to what a bird can hold or carry. Because of this, a bird must make many trips afield to gather enough materials to complete its nest. Most nests take at least four days or more, and hundreds, if not thousands, of trips to build.

The simple **ground nest** is scraped out of the earth. A shallow depression that usually contains no nesting material, it is made by birds such as the Killdeer and Horned Lark.

Another kind of nest, the **platform nest**, represents a more complex type of nest building. Constructed of small twigs and branches, the platform nest is a simple arrangement of sticks which forms a platform and features a small depression to nestle the eggs.

Some platform nests, such as those of the Canada Goose, are constructed on the ground and are made with mud and grass. Platform nests can also be on cliffs, bridges, balconies or even in flowerpots. This kind of nest gives space to adventurous youngsters and functions as a landing platform for the parents. Many waterfowl build platform nests on the ground, usually near water or actually in water. These floating platform nests vary with the water level, thus preventing nests with eggs from being flooded. Platform nests, constructed by such birds as Mourning Doves and herons, are not anchored to the tree and may tumble from the branches during high winds and storms.

The **cup nest** is a modified platform nest, used by three-quarters of all songbirds. Constructed from the outside in, a supporting platform is constructed first. This platform is attached firmly to a tree, shrub, rock ledge or the ground. Next, the sides are constructed of grasses, small twigs, bark or leaves, which are woven together and often glued with mud for added strength. The inner cup, lined with feathers, animal fur, soft plant material or animal hair, is constructed last. The mother bird uses her chest to cast the final contours of the inner nest.

The **pendulous nest** is an unusual nest, looking more like a sock hanging from a branch than a nest. Inaccessible to most predators, these nests are attached to the end of the smallest branches of a tree and often wave wildly in the breeze. Woven very tightly of plant fibers, they are strong, watertight and take up to a week to construct. More commonly used by tropical birds, this complicated type of nest has also been mastered by orioles and kinglets. A small opening on the top or side allows the parents access to the grass-lined interior. (It must be one heck of a ride to be inside one of these nests during a windy spring thunderstorm!)

Another type of nest, the **cavity nest**, is used by many bird species, including woodpeckers and Western Bluebirds. The cavity nest is usually excavated in a tree branch or trunk and offers shelter from storms, sun, predators and cold. A relatively small entrance hole in a tree leads to an inner chamber up to 10 inches (25 cm) deep. Usually constructed by woodpeckers, the cavity nest is typically used only once by its builder but subsequently can be used for many years by other birds, such as mergansers, bluebirds and swallows, which do not have the capability of excavating one for themselves. Kingfishers, on the other hand, excavate a tunnel up to 4 feet (1 m) long, which connects the entrance in a riverbank to the nest chamber. These cavity nests are often sparsely lined because they are already well insulated.

One of the most clever of all nest types is known as the **no nest** or daycare nest. Parasitic birds, such as Brown-headed Cowbirds, build no nests at all! The egg-laden female expertly searches out other birds' nests and sneaks in to lay one of her own eggs while the host mother is not looking, thereby leaving the host mother to raise an adopted youngster. The mother cowbird wastes no energy building a nest only to have it raided by a predator. By using several nests of other birds, she spreads out her progeny so at least one of her offspring will live to maturity.

Some birds, including some swallows, take nest building one step further. They use a collection of small balls of mud to construct an adobe-style home. Constructed beneath the eaves of houses, under bridges or inside chimneys, some of these nests look like simple cup nests. Others are completely enclosed, with small tunnel-like openings that lead into a safe nesting chamber for the baby birds.

Who Builds the Nest?

In general, the female bird builds the nest. She gathers nesting materials and constructs a nest, with an occasional visit from her mate to check on progress. In some species, both parents contribute equally to the construction of a nest. A male bird might forage for precisely the right sticks, grass or mud, but it is often the female that forms or puts together the nest. She uses her body to form the egg chamber. Rarely does the male build a nest by himself.

Fledging

Fledging is the interval between hatching and flight or leaving the nest. Some birds leave the nest within hours of hatching (precocial), but it might be weeks before they are able to fly. This is common with waterfowl and shorebirds. Until they start to fly, they are called fledglings. Birds that are still in the nest are called nestlings. Other baby birds are born naked and blind, and remain in the nest for several weeks (altricial).

Why Birds Migrate

Why do birds migrate? The short answer is simple–food. Birds migrate to areas with high concentrations of food, as it is easier to breed where food is than where it is not. A typical migrator–the Barn Swallow, for instance–will migrate from the tropics as far south as South America to nest in North America, taking advantage of billions of newly hatched insects to feed its young. This trip is called **complete migration**.

Some birds of prey return from their complete migration to northern regions that are overflowing with small rodents, such as mice and voles, that have continued to breed in winter.

Complete migrators have a set time and pattern of migration. Each year at nearly the same time, they take off and head for a specific wintering ground. Complete migrators may travel great distances, sometimes as much as 15,000 miles (24,150 km) or more in a year. But complete migration doesn't necessarily imply flying from the frozen northland to a tropical destination. The Dark-eyed Junco, for example, is a complete migrator that flies from far reaches of Canada to spend the winter in right here in Wyoming. This is still called **complete migration**.

There are many interesting aspects to complete migrators. In the spring, males usually migrate several weeks before the females, arriving early to scope out possibilities for nesting sites and food sources, and to begin to defend territories. The females arrive several weeks later. In the autumn, in many species, the females and their young leave early, often up to four weeks before the adult males.

All migrators are not the same type. **Partial migrators**, such as American Goldfinches, usually wait until their food supplies dwindle before flying south. Unlike complete migrators, partial migrators move only far enough south, or sometimes east and west, to find abundant food. In some years it might be only a few hundred miles, while in other years it might be nearly a thousand. This kind of migration, dependent on weather and the availability of food, is sometimes called seasonal movement.

Unlike the predictable ebbing and flowing behavior of complete migrators or partial migrators, **irruptive migrators** can move every third to fifth year or, in some cases, in consecutive years. These migrations are triggered when times are really tough and food is scarce. Evening Grosbeaks are an example of irruptive migrators, because they leave their normal northern range in search of food or in response to overpopulation.

How Do Birds Migrate?

One of the many secrets of migration is fat. While we humans are fighting the battle of the bulge, birds intentionally gorge themselves to put on as much fat as possible while still being able to fly. Fat provides the greatest amount of energy per unit of weight, and in the same way that your car needs gas, birds are propelled by fat and stalled without it.

During long migratory flights, fat deposits are used up quickly, and birds need to stop to "refuel." This is when backyard bird feeding stations and undeveloped, natural spaces around our towns and cities are especially important. Some birds require up to 2-3 days of constant feeding to build their fat reserves before continuing their seasonal trip.

Some birds, such as most eagles, hawks, ospreys, falcons and vultures, migrate during the day. Larger birds can hold more body fat, go longer without eating and take longer to migrate. These birds glide along on rising columns of warm air, called thermals, which hold them aloft while they slowly make their way north or south. They generally rest during the night and hunt early in the morning before the sun has a chance to warm the land and create good soaring conditions. Birds migrating during the day use a combination of landforms, rivers, and the rising and setting sun to guide them in the right direction.

Most other birds migrate during the night. Studies show that some birds which migrate at night use the stars to navigate. Others use the setting sun, while still others, such as doves, use the earth's magnetic fields to guide them north or south. While flying at night might seem like a crazy idea, nocturnal migration is safer for several reasons. First, there are fewer nighttime predators for migrating birds. Second, traveling at night allows time during the day to find food in unfamiliar surroundings. Finally, nighttime wind patterns tend to be flat, or laminar. These flat winds don't have the turbulence associated with daytime winds and can actually help carry smaller birds by pushing them along.

HOW TO USE THIS GUIDE

To help you quickly and easily identify birds, this field guide is organized by color. Simply note the color of the bird and turn to that section. Refer to the first page for the color key. The Williamson's Sapsucker, for example, is black and white with a yellow belly. Because this bird is mostly black and white, it will be found in the black and white section. Each color section is also arranged by size, generally with the smaller birds first. Sections may also incorporate the average size in a range, which, in some cases, reflects size differences between male and female birds. Flip through the pages in that color section to find the bird. If you already know the name of the bird, check the index for the page number. In some species, the male and female are remarkably different in color. In others, the color of breeding and winter plumages differs. These species will have an inset photograph with a page reference and, in most cases, are found in two color sections.

In the description section you will find a variety of information about the bird. On page 21 is a sample of information included in the book.

Range Maps

Range maps are included for each bird. Colored areas indicate where in Wyoming a particular bird is most likely to be found. The colors represent the presence of a species during a specific season, not the density or amount of birds in the area. Green is used for summer, blue for winter, red for year-round and yellow for areas where the bird is seen during migration. While every effort has been made to accurately depict these ranges, they are only general guidelines. Ranges actually change on an ongoing basis due to a variety of factors. Changes in weather, species abundance, landscape and vital resources, such as availability of food and water, can affect local populations, migration and movements, causing birds to be found in areas that are atypical for the species.

Colored areas simply mean bird sightings for that species have been frequent in those areas and less frequent in others. Please use the maps as intended–as general guides only.

Birds in Yellowstone and Grand Teton National Parks

In the upper left corner of each range map is a bold outline that defines the borders of Yellowstone and Grand Teton National Parks. These parks are specially marked to help you see and identify more birds in Yellowstone and the Tetons during your visits.

Nearly all birds in this field guide are found in the parks. While most are common throughout the parks, some are more easily spotted at specific locations. In these cases, special information has been added to Stan's Notes that points out the best places in the parks to see the birds.

In addition, at the bottom of these pages you will notice an illustration of a group of trees. This icon will help you quickly find the pages with extra information relative to the birds found in Yellowstone and Grand Teton National Parks.

Common Name

YEAR-ROUND
MIGRATION
SUMMER
WINTER
PARKS

Size: measures head to tail, may include wingspan

Male: a brief description of the male bird, and may include breeding, winter or other plumages

Female: a brief description of the female bird, which is sometimes not the same as the male

Juvenile: a brief description of the juvenile bird, which often looks like the female

Nest: the kind of nest this bird builds to raise its young; who builds the nest; how many broods per year

Eggs: how many eggs you might expect to see in a nest; color and marking

Incubation: the average time parents spend incubating the eggs; who does the incubation

Fledging: the average time young spend in the nest after hatching but before they leave the nest; who does the most "childcare" and feeding

Migration: complete (consistent, seasonal), partial (seasonal movement, destination varies), irruptive (unpredictable, depends on the food supply), non-migrator; additional comments

Food: what the bird eats most of the time (e.g., seeds, insects, fruit, nectar, small mammals, fish); if it typically comes to a bird feeding station

Compare: notes about other birds that look similar, and the pages on which they can be found, may include extra information to help identify

Stan's Notes: Interesting gee-whiz natural history information. This could be something to look or listen for, or something to help positively identify the bird. Also includes remarkable features.

Pages with this icon include special information in Stan's Notes about where to find the bird in Yellowstone and Grand Teton National Parks. 21

male

female
pg. 329

Bobolink
Dolichonyx oryzivorus

MIGRATION
SUMMER

Size: 7" (18 cm)

Male: Nearly all-black bird with a black chest and belly. Pale yellow on back of head and nape of neck. White patch on wings and rump.

Female: pale yellow with dark brown stripes on the head, thin dark line extends through the eye, dark streaks on back and sides

Juvenile: similar to female, lacking dark streaks

Nest: ground; scraped-out depression lined with grass; 1 brood per year

Eggs: 4-6; gray to red brown with brown markings

Incubation: 10-13 days; female incubates

Fledging: 10-14 days; female and male feed young

Migration: complete, to South America, mostly Brazil

Food: insects, seeds

Compare: Male Bobolink is similar in size to the male Red-winged Blackbird (pg. 31), but lacks the red and yellow wing bars. Look for yellow on the head, a white patch on the wings and the black belly of male Bobolink.

Stan's Notes: A member of the blackbird family. Closely related to meadowlarks. A common bird of prairies, grasslands and open fields. In spring, the male will perch on plant stems and repeat its bubbling "bob-o-link" song (which provided the common name). Gives a loud, repeated "ink" whistle during flight. When disturbed, the female will run from her highly concealed ground nest before taking flight. By late summer, the males will have molted to a drab color similar to the females.

23

female
pg. 131

male

Brown-headed Cowbird
Molothrus ater

SUMMER

Size: 7½" (19 cm)

Male: Glossy black bird, reminiscent of a male Red-winged Blackbird. Head is chocolate brown. Pointed, sharp gray bill. Dark eyes.

Female: dull brown bird, bill similar to the male bill

Juvenile: similar to female, but dull gray color and has a streaked chest

Nest: no nest; lays eggs in the nests of other birds

Eggs: 5-7; white with brown markings

Incubation: 10-13 days; host bird incubates eggs

Fledging: 10-11 days; host birds feed young

Migration: complete, to southwestern states

Food: insects, seeds; will come to seed feeders

Compare: The male Red-winged Blackbird (pg. 31) is slightly larger with red and yellow patches on its upper wings. Common Grackle (pg. 39) has a long tail and lacks the brown head. The European Starling (pg. 27) has a shorter tail.

Stan's Notes: A blackbird family member. Of about 750 species of parasitic birds worldwide, this is the only parasitic bird in the state, laying eggs in host birds' nests, leaving others to raise its young. Cowbirds are known to have laid eggs in the nests of over 200 species of birds. Some birds reject cowbird eggs, but most will incubate them and raise the young, even to the exclusion of their own. Look for warblers and other birds feeding young birds twice their own size. Flocks of cowbirds follow herds of bison in both parks; look for them landing on the backs of bison and other large animals. Seen in busier parts of Yellowstone, such as Old Faithful.

winter

breeding

European Starling
Sturnus vulgaris

YEAR-ROUND

Size: 7½" (19 cm)

Male: Gray-to-black bird with white speckles in fall and winter. Shiny purple black during spring and summer. Long, pointed yellow bill in spring turns gray in fall. Short tail.

Female: same as male

Juvenile: similar to adult, gray brown in color with a streaked chest

Nest: cavity; male and female line cavity; 2 broods per year

Eggs: 4-6; bluish with brown markings

Incubation: 12-14 days; female and male incubate

Fledging: 18-20 days; female and male feed young

Migration: non-migrator to partial; will move around to find food

Food: insects, seeds, fruit; will come to seed and suet feeders

Compare: Similar to the Common Grackle (pg. 39), but lacks its long tail. The male Brown-headed Cowbird (pg. 25) is the same size, but it has a brown head and longer tail.

Stan's Notes: A great songster, this bird can mimic other birds and sounds. Often displaces woodpeckers, chickadees and other cavity-nesting birds. Can be very aggressive and destroy eggs or young of other birds. Jaws are designed to be the most powerful when opening; the birds can pry crevices apart to locate hidden insects. Bill changes color with the seasons: yellow in spring, gray in autumn. Gathers in the hundreds in autumn. Not a native bird, it was introduced to New York City in 1890-91 from Europe.

female
pg. 139

male

Spotted Towhee
Pipilo maculatus

SUMMER

Size: 8½" (22 cm)

Male: Mostly black with dirty red-brown sides and a white belly. Multiple white spots on wings and sides. A long black tail with a white tip. Rich red eyes.

Female: very similar to male, with a brown head

Juvenile: brown with a heavily streaked chest

Nest: cup; female builds; 1-2 broods per year

Eggs: 3-5; white with brown markings

Incubation: 12-14 days; female and male incubate

Fledging: 10-12 days; female and male feed young

Migration: complete, to southwestern states

Food: seeds, fruit, insects; will visit feeders

Compare: The Green-tailed Towhee (pg. 281) is closely related, but it lacks the bold black and red of the male Spotted. Male Bobolink (pg. 23) has a black belly and is pale yellow on the back of the head and nape of neck.

Stan's Notes: Inhabits a variety of habitats, from thick brush and forests to suburban backyards. Often scratches noisily through dead leaves on the ground for food; more than 70 percent of its diet is plant material. Eats more insects during spring and summer. Well known for retreating from danger by walking away rather than taking to flight. Cup nest is nearly always on the ground under bushes but away from where the male perches to sing. Begins breeding in April. Lays eggs in May. After breeding season, moves to higher elevations. Song and plumage vary geographically.

female
pg. 141

male

Red-winged Blackbird
Agelaius phoeniceus

YEAR-ROUND
SUMMER

Size: 8½" (22 cm)

Male: Jet-black bird with red and yellow shoulder patches on upper wings. Pointed black bill.

Female: heavily streaked brown bird with a pointed brown bill and white eyebrows

Juvenile: same as female

Nest: cup; female builds; 2-3 broods per year

Eggs: 3-4; bluish green with brown markings

Incubation: 10-12 days; female incubates

Fledging: 11-14 days; female and male feed young

Migration: complete to non-migrator in Wyoming

Food: seeds, insects; will come to seed feeders

Compare: Slightly larger than the male Brown-headed Cowbird (pg. 25), but is less iridescent and lacks the Cowbird's brown head. Differs from all other blackbirds due to the red and yellow patches on its wings (epaulets).

Stan's Notes: It's a sure sign of spring when the Red-wings return to the marshes. Flocks with as many as 10,000 birds have been reported. Males arrive before females and defend their territories by singing from the top of surrounding vegetation. Male repeats his call from cattail tops while showing off his red and yellow shoulder patches. Female chooses a mate and often nests over shallow water in thick stands of cattails. Can be aggressive when defending the nest. Feeds mostly on seeds during fall and spring, switching to insects in summer.

female pg. 145

Brewer's Blackbird
Euphagus cyanocephalus

SUMMER

Size: 9" (22.5 cm)

Male: Overall glossy black, shining green in direct light. Head is more purple than green. Bright white or pale yellow eyes. Winter plumage can be dull gray to black.

Female: similar to male, only overall grayish brown, most have dark eyes

Juvenile: similar to female

Nest: cup; female builds; 1-2 broods per year

Eggs: 4-6; gray with brown markings

Incubation: 12-14 days; female incubates

Fledging: 13-14 days; female and male feed young

Migration: complete, to southwestern states

Food: insects, seeds, fruit

Compare: Smaller than the Common Grackle (pg. 39), lacking the long tail. Male Brown-headed Cowbird (pg. 25) is smaller and has a brown head. Male Red-winged Blackbird (pg. 31) has red and yellow shoulder marks.

Stan's Notes: Often in fields and open places such as wet pastures and mountain meadows up to 10,000 feet (3,050 m). Males and some females are easily identified by their bright, nearly white eyes. A cowbird host. Usually nests in a shrub, small tree or on ground. Prefers to nest in small colonies of up to 20 pairs. Doesn't get along with Common Grackles; often driven out of the nest area by the expansion of grackles. Gathers in large flocks to migrate with Brown-headed Cowbirds, Red-winged Blackbirds and other blackbirds. Expanding its range in North America.

female
pg. 147

male

Yellow-headed Blackbird
Xanthocephalus xanthocephalus

SUMMER

Size: 9-11" (22.5-28 cm)

Male: A large black bird with a lemon yellow head, breast and nape of neck. Black mask and gray bill. White wing patches.

Female: similar to male, only slightly smaller with a brown body and dull yellow head and chest

Juvenile: similar to female

Nest: cup; female builds; 2 broods per year

Eggs: 3-5; greenish white with brown markings

Incubation: 11-13 days; female incubates

Fledging: 9-12 days; female feeds young

Migration: complete, to southwestern states and Mexico

Food: insects, seeds; will come to ground feeders

Compare: Larger than the male Red-winged Blackbird (pg. 31), which has red and yellow patches on its wings. Male Yellow-headed is the only large black bird with a bright yellow head.

Stan's Notes: Usually heard before seen; the call is low, hoarse, raspy or metallic-sounding. Nests in deep water marshes unlike its cousin, the Red-winged Blackbird, which prefers shallow water. The male gives an impressive mating display, flying with his head drooped and feet and tail pointing down while steadily beating his wings. Female incubates alone and feeds 3-5 young. Young keep low and out of sight for up to three weeks before starting to fly. Migrates in flocks of up to 200 with other blackbirds. Flocks made up mainly of males return first in early April; females return later. Most colonies consist of 20-100 nests. Nests in lower elevations, such as in the ponds of Junction Butte, east of Yellowstone Bridge.

in flight

Black Tern
Chlidonias niger

SUMMER

Size: 10" (25 cm)

Male: Breeding plumage head, neck and body are black. Gray back, wings and tail. Dark eyes, bill and legs. Winter plumage is overall gray with a nearly white head and white undertail. Pale yellow legs.

Female: same as male

Juvenile: similar to winter adult, back is more brown than gray

Nest: floating platform; male and female construct; 1-2 broods per year

Eggs: 2-4; green with brown markings

Incubation: 21-22 days; female and male incubate

Fledging: 21-28 days; male and female feed young

Migration: complete, to South America

Food: insects, small fish, aquatic insects

Compare: The only tern with a black head and body.

Stan's Notes: Common breeding bird in wetlands from March to September, nesting in small colonies. Nest is often just a floating mat of vegetation. Often will use an old grebe nest. Young females begin to breed at 2 years of age. Aggressively defends the nest site and young. Will dive at intruders and predators. Has a unique buoyant flight pattern, with erratic swoops. Unlike other species of terns, rarely plunges into water after prey. Hunts for insects on the surface of ponds and marshes and picks insects out of the air. Occasionally follows plows to pick off insects disturbed in fields. Gives a sharp "keff" call while in flight. Migrates in large flocks.

Common Grackle

Quiscalus quiscula

SUMMER

Size: 11-13" (28-33 cm)

Male: Large black bird with an iridescent blue black head, a purple brown body, long black tail, long thin bill and bright golden eyes.

Female: similar to male, only duller and smaller

Juvenile: similar to female

Nest: cup; female builds; 2 broods per year

Eggs: 4-5; greenish white with brown markings

Incubation: 13-14 days; female incubates

Fledging: 16-20 days; female and male feed young

Migration: complete, to southwestern states

Food: fruit, seeds, insects; comes to seed feeders

Compare: European Starling (pg. 27) is much smaller with a speckled appearance, and has a yellow bill during breeding season. Male Red-winged Blackbird (pg. 31) has red and yellow wing markings (epaulets).

Stan's Notes: Usually nests in small colonies of up to 75 pairs but travels with other blackbird species in large flocks. Known to feed in farmers' fields. The common name is derived from the Latin word *graculus*, meaning "to cough," for its loud raspy call. Male holds tail in a deep V shape during flight. The flight pattern is usually level, as opposed to an undulating up-and-down movement. Unlike most birds, it has larger muscles for opening the mouth (rather than for closing it) and prying crevices apart to locate hidden insects.

American Coot
Fulica americana

YEAR-ROUND
SUMMER

Size: 13-16" (33-40 cm)

Male: Slate gray to black all over. White bill with a dark band near the tip. Green legs and feet. A small white patch near the base of the tail. Prominent red eyes. A small red patch above the bill between the eyes.

Female: same as male

Juvenile: much paler than adult, with a gray bill and same white rump patch

Nest: floating platform; female and male build; 1 brood per year

Eggs: 9-12; pinkish buff with brown markings

Incubation: 21-25 days; female and male incubate

Fledging: 49-52 days; female and male feed young

Migration: complete to non-migrator in Wyoming

Food: insects, aquatic plants

Compare: Smaller than most other waterfowl. This is the only black water bird or duck-like bird with a white bill.

Stan's Notes: An excellent diver and swimmer, typically seen in large flocks on open water. Not a duck, as it doesn't have webbed feet, but large lobed toes instead. At takeoff, scrambles across the surface of water with wings flapping. Bobs head while swimming. Anchors its floating nest to plants. Huge flocks of up to 1,000 birds gather for migration. The name "Coot" is of unknown origin, but in Middle English, *coote* described various waterfowl. Also called Mud Hen. A favorite food of Bald Eagles. Seen in lower elevation ponds and potholes, such as in Junction Butte, and in the small lake called Floating Island Lake near the road in the Tower area.

in flight

American Crow
Corvus brachyrhynchos

YEAR-ROUND

Size: 18" (45 cm)

Male: All-black bird with black bill, legs and feet. Can have a purple sheen in direct sunlight.

Female: same as male

Juvenile: same as adult

Nest: platform; female builds; 1 brood per year

Eggs: 4-6; bluish to olive green with brown marks

Incubation: 18 days; female incubates

Fledging: 28-35 days; female and male feed young

Migration: non-migrator; moves around to find food

Food: fruit, insects, mammals, fish, carrion; will come to seed and suet feeders

Compare: The Common Raven (pg. 45) has a larger bill, shaggy throat feathers and a deep, raspy call; Crow has a higher-pitched call. Raven has a wedge-shaped tail, apparent in flight; Crow has a squared tail.

Stan's Notes: One of the most recognizable birds in Wyoming. Often reuses its nest every year if not taken over by a Great Horned Owl. Collects and stores bright, shiny objects in the nest. Mimics other birds and human voices. One of the smartest of all birds and very social, often entertaining itself by provoking chases with other birds. Eats roadkill but rarely hit by vehicles. Can live up to 20 years. Unmated birds, called helpers, help raise the young. Large extended families roost together at night, dispersing daily to hunt. Can be found just about everywhere in both parks. Many of the pull-out parking areas have both crows and ravens patrolling them, looking for any handouts from tourists.

in flight

Common Raven
Corvus corax

YEAR-ROUND

Size: 22-27" (56-69 cm)

Male: Large all-black bird. Large black bill, shaggy beard of feathers on throat and chin, and a large wedge-shaped tail, as seen in flight.

Female: same as male

Juvenile: same as adult

Nest: platform; female and male construct; 1 brood per year

Eggs: 4-6; pale green with brown markings

Incubation: 18-21 days; female incubates

Fledging: 38-44 days; female and male feed young

Migration: non-migrator; moves around to find food

Food: insects, fruit, small animals, carrion; will come to feeders

Compare: Larger than its cousin, the American Crow (pg. 43), which lacks shaggy throat feathers. Glides on flat, outstretched wings unlike the slight V-shaped wing pattern of the Crow. Listen for the Raven's deep, low raspy call to distinguish it from the higher-pitched Crow.

Stan's Notes: Considered by some people to be the smartest of all birds. Known for its aerial acrobatics and long swooping dives. Sometimes scavenges with crows and gulls. A cooperative hunter that often communicates the location of a good source of food to other ravens. Complex courtship includes grabbing bills, preening each other and cooing. Most begin to breed at 3-4 years. Mates are long-term. Uses the same nest site for many years. Seen nearly everywhere in both parks. Many of the pull-out parking areas have ravens and crows patrolling for handouts from tourists.

45

soaring

juvenile

Turkey Vulture
Cathartes aura

SUMMER

Size: 26-32" (66-80 cm); up to 6-foot wingspan

Male: Large bird with an obvious red head and legs. In flight, the wings appear two-toned: black leading edge with gray on the trailing edge and tip. The tips of wings end in finger-like projections. Long squared tail. Ivory bill.

Female: same as male

Juvenile: similar to adult, with a gray-to-blackish head and bill

Nest: no nest, or minimal nest on a cliff or in a cave; 1 brood per year

Eggs: 1-3; white with brown markings

Incubation: 38-41 days; female and male incubate

Fledging: 66-88 days; female and male feed young

Migration: complete, to southwestern states, Mexico and Central and South America

Food: carrion; parents regurgitate for young

Compare: Bald Eagle (pg. 83) is larger and lacks two-toned wings. Unlike the Bald Eagle, Turkey Vulture holds its wings in a slight V shape during flight.

Stan's Notes: The vulture's naked head is an adaptation to reduce risk of feather fouling (picking up diseases) from carcasses. Unlike hawks and eagles, it has weak feet more suited to walking than grasping. One of the few birds that has a developed sense of smell. Mostly mute, making only grunts and groans. Seen in trees with wings outstretched, sunning itself.

in flight

juvenile

crests

drying

Double-crested Cormorant
Phalacrocorax auritus

SUMMER

Size: 33" (84 cm); up to 4⅓-foot wingspan

Male: Large black water bird with a long snake-like neck. Long gray bill with yellow at the base and a hooked tip.

Female: same as male

Juvenile: lighter brown with a grayish chest and neck

Nest: platform, in a colony; male and female build; 1 brood per year

Eggs: 3-4; bluish white without markings

Incubation: 25-29 days; female and male incubate

Fledging: 37-42 days; male and female feed young

Migration: complete, to southwestern states, Mexico and Central America

Food: small fish, aquatic insects

Compare: Turkey Vulture (pg. 47) is similar in size and also perches on branches with wings open to dry in the sun, but it has a naked red head. American Coot (pg. 41) lacks the long neck and long pointed bill.

Stan's Notes: Often seen flying in a large V formation. Usually roosts in large groups in trees near water. Swims underwater to catch fish, holding its wings at its sides. Lacks the oil gland that keeps feathers from becoming waterlogged. To dry off, it strikes an erect pose with wings outstretched, facing the sun. The common name refers to the two crests on its head, which are not usually seen. "Cormorant" comes from the Latin words *corvus*, meaning "crow," and *L. marinus*, meaning "pertaining to the sea," literally, "Sea Crow."

49

male

female

Downy Woodpecker
Dryobates pubescens

YEAR-ROUND

Size: 6" (15 cm)

Male: A small woodpecker with an all-white belly, black-and-white spotted wings, a black line running through the eyes, a short black bill, a white stripe down the back and red mark on the back of the head. Several small black spots along the sides of white tail.

Female: same as male, but lacks a red mark on head

Juvenile: same as female, some have a red mark near the forehead

Nest: cavity; male and female excavate; 1 brood per year

Eggs: 3-5; white without markings

Incubation: 11-12 days; female and male incubate, female incubates during the day, male at night

Fledging: 20-25 days; male and female feed young

Migration: non-migrator

Food: insects, seeds; visits seed and suet feeders

Compare: Nearly identical to the Hairy Woodpecker (pg. 61), but smaller. Look for the shorter, thinner bill to help identify the Downy.

Stan's Notes: Abundant and widespread where trees are present, and perhaps the most common woodpecker in the United States. Stiff tail feathers help brace it like a tripod as it clings to a tree. Like other woodpeckers, it has a long, barbed tongue to pull insects from tiny places. Male and female drum on branches or hollow logs to announce territory, which is rarely larger than 5 acres (2 ha). Male performs most of the brooding. Will winter roost in cavity. Doesn't breed in high elevations but often moves there in winter for food.

female pg. 121

male

non-breeding
male

Lark Bunting
Calamospiza melanocorys

MIGRATION
SUMMER

Size: 6½" (16 cm)

Male: A short, stocky black bird with a large broad head, white wing patches and large bluish gray bill. Winter is black, brown, gray and white-striped with white wing patches.

Female: overall brown with a heavily streaked breast, white belly and black vertical line on each side of a white chin, may have a dark central spot on the breast, faint white eyebrows

Juvenile: similar to adult of the same sex

Nest: cup; female builds; 1-2 broods per year

Eggs: 4-6; pale blue with markings

Incubation: 11-13 days; female and male incubate

Fledging: 8-12 days; female and male feed young

Migration: complete, to southwestern states and Mexico

Food: insects, seeds

Compare: The bold black and white plumage of the breeding male is hard to confuse with any other bird's. Look for the rather large, broad head and large bill to help identify the male Lark Bunting.

Stan's Notes: Common in the dry plains and sagebrush regions of Wyoming. Male flashes white wing patches on his short, rounded wings while flying with shallow wing beats. Male takes to the air to display to the female, setting his wings in a V position and floating back, rocking like a butterfly, singing a most amazing song. Song is like that of Old World larks, hence the common name. Will flock in autumn with hundreds, if not thousands, of other Lark Buntings for migration.

male

winter
male

winter
female

Snow Bunting
Plectrophenax nivalis

WINTER

Size: 7" (18 cm)

Male: Winter plumage bunting has a white chin, breast and belly. Rusty brown head, back and shoulders. Small yellow bill. Black legs and feet. Breeding plumage is overall white with black and white wings.

Female: similar to winter male, with less black

Juvenile: similar to winter adults

Nest: cavity; female builds; 1-2 broods per year

Eggs: 4-7; green to blue with brown markings

Incubation: 10-16 days; female incubates

Fledging: 10-17 days; male and female feed young

Migration: complete, to Wyoming and northern states

Food: insects, seeds

Compare: This bird is easy to identify because no other small sparrow-like bird has so much white.

Stan's Notes: A winter resident of Wyoming. Often feeds on the ground along roads. Usually seen in flocks of up to 30 individuals of mixed ages and sexes. Individual Snow Buntings appear slightly different from each other; some are completely black and white, others are a combination of black, white, brown and rust. Winter plumage is seen from September to March. Sometimes seen with Horned Larks. Female builds her nest with grass and moss in a cavity or on a cliff that is well protected from the weather. Young hatch at different times, so some leave the nest before others.

male

female

Red-naped Sapsucker
Sphyrapicus nuchalis

MIGRATION
SUMMER

Size: 8½" (22 cm)

Male: Black-and-white pattern on the back in two rows. Red forehead, chin and nape of neck.

Female: same as male, but has a white chin and more white on the back

Juvenile: brown version of adults, lacking any of the red markings

Nest: cavity; female and male excavate; 1 brood per year

Eggs: 3-7; pale white without markings

Incubation: 12-13 days; female and male incubate

Fledging: 25-29 days; female and male feed young

Migration: complete, to southwestern states, Mexico and Central America

Food: insects, tree sap; will visit feeders

Compare: The Lewis's Woodpecker (pg. 283) lacks the black-and-white pattern of the Red-naped.

Stan's Notes: Closely related to the Yellow-bellied Sapsucker of the eastern U.S. Often associated with aspen, cottonwood and willow trees, nearly always nesting in aspen trees where they are present. Creates several horizontal rows of holes in a tree from which sap oozes. A wide variety of birds and animals use the sap wells that sapsuckers drill. Sapsuckers lap the sap and eat the insects that are also attracted to sap. Cannot suck sap as the name implies; instead, they lap it with their tongues. Some females lack the white chin that helps to differentiate the sexes. Check any stands of aspen trees within the park boundaries. Areas around Pelican Bridge and Indian Lake are good places to search.

male

female

Williamson's Sapsucker

Sphyrapicus thyroideus

MIGRATION
SUMMER

Size: 9" (22.5 cm)

Male: More black than white with a red chin and bright yellow belly. Bold white stripes just above and below the eyes. White rump and wing patches flash during flight.

Female: finely barred black-and-white back, a brown head, yellow belly and no wing patches

Juvenile: similar to female

Nest: cavity; male excavates; 1 brood per year

Eggs: 3-7; pale white without markings

Incubation: 12-14 days; male and female incubate

Fledging: 21-28 days; female and male feed young

Migration: complete, to Mexico and Central America

Food: insects, tree sap; will visit feeders

Compare: Lewis's Woodpecker (pg. 283) has a red face and belly. Female Williamson's is similar to the Northern Flicker (pg. 155), but Flicker has a gray head and brown and black back.

Stan's Notes: Largest sapsucker species with a striking difference between the male and female. Male drums early in spring to attract a mate and claim territory. Like the drumming of other sapsuckers, Williamson's drumming has an irregular cadence. Male excavates a new cavity each year, frequently in the same tree. Male does more incubating than the female. Occupies coniferous forests, foraging for insects and drilling uniform rows of holes from which tree sap oozes. Feeds upon the sap and the insects that are attracted to it. Warblers and other bird species also feed from these taps. Sap wells are nearly exclusively in conifers.

male

female

Hairy Woodpecker
Dryobates villosus

YEAR-ROUND

Size: 9" (22.5 cm)

Male: A black-and-white woodpecker with a white belly. Black wings with rows of white spots. White stripe down the back. Long black bill. Red mark on back of head.

Female: same as male, but lacks a red mark on head

Juvenile: grayer version of female

Nest: cavity; female and male excavate; 1 brood per year

Eggs: 3-6; white without markings

Incubation: 11-15 days; female and male incubate, female incubates during the day, male at night

Fledging: 28-30 days; male and female feed young

Migration: non-migrator

Food: insects, nuts, seeds; will come to seed and suet feeders

Compare: Larger than Downy Woodpecker (pg. 51), with a longer bill nearly the width of its head.

Stan's Notes: A common woodpecker of wooded backyards that announces its arrival with a sharp chirp before landing on feeders. This bird is responsible for eating many destructive forest insects. Has a barbed tongue, which helps it extract insects from trees. Tiny bristle-like feathers at the base of bill protect the nostrils from wood dust. Drums on hollow logs, branches or stovepipes in spring to announce its territory. Often prefers to excavate nest cavities in live aspen trees. Has a larger, more oval cavity entrance than that of the Downy. Trees around any park stores and campgrounds are good places to see woodpeckers. Check Tower Fall and Mammoth.

winter

breeding

Eared Grebe
Podiceps nigricollis

SUMMER

Size: 13" (33 cm)

Male: Breeding plumage head, neck and back are overall dark brown to black. Chestnut brown sides and chest. Wispy yellow plumes feather out behind red eyes. Small black bill. Winter plumage chin and sides are dirty brown to black and white. Red eyes and a dark-tipped gray bill.

Female: same as male

Juvenile: similar to winter adult

Nest: floating platform; female and male construct; 1-2 broods per year

Eggs: 3-5; light blue with brown markings

Incubation: 20-22 days; female and male incubate

Fledging: 20-40 days; male and female teach the young what to eat

Migration: complete, to the Gulf Coast and Mexico

Food: fish, aquatic insects

Compare: American Coot (pg. 41) has a large white bill. Western Grebe (pg. 79) has a long yellow bill.

Stan's Notes: A grebe of pothole lakes and ponds, nesting in large colonies. Constructs a platform nest in shallow water, made from reeds and grasses. Often builds more than one nest. Breeds from April to August. A few days after hatching, young are fed small feathers. The feathers pad the stomach and are thought to aid in the digestion of fish and fish bones. Chick siblings are not the same size, because young hatch several days apart. Chicks ride on the backs of parents. Often dives underwater to avoid danger, staying submerged with just its bill above the surface.

Black-necked Stilt

Himantopus mexicanus

MIGRATION
SUMMER

Size: 14" (36 cm)

Male: Upper parts of the head, neck and back are black. Lower parts are white. Ridiculously long red-to-pink legs. Long black bill.

Female: similar to male, only browner on back

Juvenile: similar to female, brown instead of black

Nest: ground; female and male construct; 1 brood per year

Eggs: 3-5; off-white with dark markings

Incubation: 22-26 days; female and male incubate, male incubates during the day, female at night

Fledging: 28-32 days; female and male feed young

Migration: complete, to southwestern states, Mexico and Central and South America

Food: aquatic insects

Compare: The outrageous length of the red-to-pink legs make this shorebird hard to confuse with any other species.

Stan's Notes: This is a breeding bird and migrator in Wyoming. Nests alone or in small colonies in open areas. A very vocal bird of shallow marshes, giving a "kek-kek-kek" call. Its legs are up to 10 inches (25 cm) long and may be the longest in the bird world in proportion to the body. Known to transport water with water-soaked belly feathers (belly-soaking) to cool its eggs when the weather is hot. Aggressively defends its nest, eggs and young. Young leave the nest shortly after hatching.

female pg. 161

male

Bufflehead
Bucephala albeola

YEAR-ROUND
MIGRATION
WINTER

Size: 13-15" (33-38 cm)

Male: A small duck with striking white sides and black back. Green purple head with a large white bonnet-like patch.

Female: brown version of male, with a brown head and white patch on cheek, just behind eyes

Juvenile: similar to female

Nest: cavity; female lines an old woodpecker cavity; 1 brood per year

Eggs: 8-10; ivory to olive without markings

Incubation: 29-31 days; female incubates

Fledging: 50-55 days; female leads young to food

Migration: partial to non-migrator in Wyoming

Food: aquatic insects

Compare: A small black and white diving duck. Look for the green purple head with a large white patch to help identify the male Bufflehead.

Stan's Notes: This very small, common duck is almost always in small groups or with other ducks. Seen on rivers and lakes in the state. Nests in old woodpecker holes. Known to use a burrow in an earthen bank when tree cavities are scarce. Will use a nest box. Uses down feathers to line the nest cavity. Unlike other ducks, the young remain in the nest for up to two days before venturing out with their mothers. Female is very territorial and stays with the same mate for many years. Found at many of the larger bodies of water in the parks. Check Fishing and Pelican Bridges. This is a diving duck, spending a couple minutes underwater, so be sure to watch for it long enough.

female pg. 171

male

Lesser Scaup
Aythya affinis

MIGRATION
SUMMER

Size: 16-17" (40-43 cm)

Male: Appears mostly black with bold white sides and a gray back. Chest and head look nearly black, but head appears purple with green highlights in direct sun. Bright yellow eyes.

Female: overall brown with a dull white patch at the base of a light gray bill, yellow eyes

Juvenile: same as female

Nest: ground; female builds; 1 brood per year

Eggs: 8-14; olive buff without markings

Incubation: 22-28 days; female incubates

Fledging: 45-50 days; female teaches young to feed

Migration: complete, to southwestern states, Mexico and Central America

Food: aquatic plants and insects

Compare: The male Common Goldeneye (pg. 73) has a white chest. Male Blue-winged Teal (pg. 167) is slightly smaller and has a white crescent on its bill. Look for bold white sides and a gray back to help identify the male Lesser Scaup.

Stan's Notes: A common diving duck. Often seen in large flocks on lakes, ponds and sewage lagoons. Submerges itself completely to feed on the bottom of lakes (unlike dabbling ducks, which only tip forward to reach the bottom). Note the bold white stripe under the wings when in flight. Male leaves the female when she starts incubating eggs. The quantity of eggs (clutch size) increases with the age of the female. This species has an interesting baby-sitting arrangement in which groups of young (crèches) are tended by 1-3 adult females. Check Junction Butte Ponds.

winter

breeding

American Avocet

Recurvirostra americana

MIGRATION
SUMMER

Size: 18" (45 cm)

Male: Black and white back, with a white belly. A long, thin upturned bill and long gray legs. Rusty red head and neck during breeding season, gray in winter.

Female: similar to male, more strongly upturned bill

Juvenile: similar to adults, slight wash of rusty red on the neck and head

Nest: ground; female and male construct; 1 brood per year

Eggs: 3-5; light olive with brown markings

Incubation: 22-29 days; female and male incubate

Fledging: 28-35 days; female and male feed young

Migration: complete, to Mexico

Food: insects, crustaceans, aquatic vegetation, fruit

Compare: One of the few long-legged shorebirds in Wyoming. The White-faced Ibis (pg. 205) is larger and has a down-curved bill. Look for the rusty red head of breeding Avocet and the long upturned bill.

Stan's Notes: A handsome, long-legged bird that is well adapted to western U.S. arid conditions. Prefers shallow alkaline, saline or brackish water. Uses its upturned bill to sweep from side to side across mud bottoms in search of insects. Both the male and female have a brood patch to incubate eggs and brood their young. Nests in loose colonies of up to 20 pairs; all members defend against intruders together. Check shallow ponds in western Yellowstone, such as the Pelican Creek Bridge and Fishing Bridge areas.

female pg. 185

male

Common Goldeneye
Bucephala clangula

WINTER

Size: 18½-20" (47-50 cm)

Male: A mostly white duck with a black back and large, puffy green head. Large white spot in front of each bright golden eye. Dark bill.

Female: large dark brown head, gray body, white collar, bright golden eyes and yellow-tipped dark bill

Juvenile: same as female, but has a dark bill

Nest: cavity; female lines an old woodpecker cavity; 1 brood per year

Eggs: 8-10; light green without markings

Incubation: 28-32 days; female incubates

Fledging: 56-59 days; female leads young to food

Migration: complete, to Wyoming, southwestern states and Mexico

Food: aquatic plants, insects, fish, mollusks

Compare: Similar to the male Lesser Scaup (pg. 69), which is smaller. Look for the white chest, golden eyes and round white spot in front of each eye to identify the male Goldeneye.

Stan's Notes: Known for its loud whistling in flight, produced by its wings. In late winter and early spring, the male often attracts a female through elaborate displays, throwing his head back while uttering a raspy note. Female will lay eggs in other goldeneye nests, resulting in some mothers incubating up to 30 eggs. Received the common name from its obvious bright golden eyes. Can be seen in both parks on larger bodies of water, such as Yellowstone Lake, Jackson Lake, Lewis Lake and Twin Lakes.

Black-billed Magpie
Pica hudsonia

YEAR-ROUND

Size: 20" (50 cm)

Male: Large black-and-white bird with a very long tail and white belly. Iridescent green wings and tail in direct sunlight. Large black bill and legs. White wing patches flash in flight.

Female: same as male

Juvenile: same as adult, but has a shorter tail

Nest: modified pendulous; male and female build; 1 brood per year

Eggs: 5-8; green with brown markings

Incubation: 16-21 days; female incubates

Fledging: 25-29 days; female and male feed young

Migration: non-migrator

Food: insects, carrion, fruit, seeds

Compare: The contrasting black-and-white colors and the very long tail of the Black-billed Magpie distinguish it from the all-black American Crow (pg. 43).

Stan's Notes: A wonderfully intelligent bird that is able to mimic dogs, cats and even people. Will often raid a barnyard dog dish for food. Feeds on a variety of food from roadkill to insects and seeds it collects from the ground. Easily identified by its bold black-and-white colors and long streaming tail. Travels in small flocks, usually family members, and tends to be very gregarious. Breeds in small colonies. Unusual dome nest (dome-shaped roof) deep within thick shrubs. Mates with same mate for several years. Prefers open fields with cattle or sheep, where it feeds on insects attracted to livestock.

non-displaying

displaying
male

female

Greater Sage-Grouse
Centrocercus urophasianus

YEAR-ROUND

Size: 26-28" (66-71 cm), male; 3-foot wingspan
20-22" (50-56 cm), female; 2½-foot wingspan

Male: Large dark gray-to-brown bird with a black chin and belly. White chest and lower neck. Yellow throat sac. Long narrow tail.

Female: uniform brown with dark barring, a black belly and pointed tail

Juvenile: similar to female

Nest: ground; female builds; 1 brood per year

Eggs: 6-12; green with reddish brown markings

Incubation: 25-27 days; female incubates

Fledging: 7-10 days; female leads young to food

Migration: non-migrator; moves around to find food

Food: insects, leaves, seeds, berries

Compare: Larger than Sharp-tailed Grouse (pg. 177), which has purple air sacs and lacks a black belly. Male Ring-necked Pheasant (pg. 211) has a red patch on its face and an obvious white ring around the neck.

Stan's Notes: The largest member of the grouse family in North America. Feeds almost exclusively on the leathery leaves of sage-brush in fall and winter, hence its common name. Each spring males gather on a traditional display ground, called a lek, to show off for the females. Displaying males lift, fan and wag their tails while leaning forward with wings drooping along their sides. They inflate a yellow air sac in the neck and make a bubbling or popping noise, which resonates from the throat.

rushing

weed dance

Clark's Grebe

Western Grebe
Aechmophorus occidentalis

SUMMER

Size: 24" (60 cm)

Male: A long-necked, nearly all-black water bird with a white chin, neck, chest and belly. Long greenish yellow bill. Bright red eyes. Dark crown extends around eyes to base of bill. In winter, becomes light gray around eyes.

Female: same as male

Juvenile: similar to adult

Nest: platform; female and male construct; 1 brood per year

Eggs: 3-4; bluish white with brown markings

Incubation: 20-23 days; female and male incubate

Fledging: 65-75 days; female and male feed young

Migration: complete, to southwestern states, the Gulf Coast and Mexico

Food: fish, aquatic insects

Compare: Striking black and white plumage makes it hard to confuse with any other bird except Clark's Grebe (see inset); nearly identical but Clark's has a bright yellow bill and white on neck and face extending above the eyes.

Stan's Notes: Well known for its unusual breeding dance, called rushing. Side by side with necks outstretched, mates spring to their webbed feet and dance across the water's surface. Often holds long stalks of water plants in bill when courting (weed dance). Shortly after choosing a large lake for breeding, it rarely flies until late in summer. Young ride on backs of adults, climbing on minutes after hatching. Nests in large colonies of up to 100 pairs on lakes with tall vegetation. Look on Lewis Lake, south of Grant Village.

soaring

Osprey
Pandion haliaetus

MIGRATION
SUMMER

Size:	21-24" (53-60 cm); up to 5½-foot wingspan
Male:	Large eagle-like bird with a white chest and belly and a nearly black back. White head with a black streak through the eyes. Large wings with black "wrist" marks. Dark bill.
Female:	same as male, but larger with a necklace of brown streaking
Juvenile:	similar to adults, with a light tan breast
Nest:	platform, often on a raised wooden platform; female and male build; 1 brood per year
Eggs:	2-4; white with brown markings
Incubation:	32-42 days; female and male incubate
Fledging:	48-58 days; male and female feed young
Migration:	complete, to southwestern states, Mexico and Central and South America
Food:	fish
Compare:	Bald Eagle (pg. 83) is on average 10 inches (25 cm) larger with an all-white head and tail. Juvenile Bald Eagle is brown with white speckles. Look for a white belly and dark stripe through the eyes to identify the Osprey.

Stan's Notes: Ospreys are in a family all their own. It is the only raptor that plunges into water feet first to catch fish. Can hover for a few seconds before diving. Carries fish in a head-first position for better aerodynamics. In flight, wings angle backward. Nests on man-made towers and in tall dead trees. Recent studies show that Ospreys mate for a long time, some perhaps for life. Once almost extinct; now doing well. Nests in many places in the parks by large lakes and rivers, especially Jackson Lake Dam.

soaring

juvenile

soaring
juvenile

Bald Eagle
Haliaeetus leucocephalus

YEAR-ROUND

Size: 31-37" (79-94 cm); up to 7½-foot wingspan

Male: Pure white head and tail contrast with a dark brown-to-black body and wings. Large, curved yellow bill and yellow feet.

Female: same as male, only slightly larger

Juvenile: dark brown with white spots or speckles throughout the body and wings, gray bill

Nest: massive platform, usually in a tree; female and male build; 1 brood per year

Eggs: 2-3; off-white without markings

Incubation: 34-36 days; female and male incubate

Fledging: 75-90 days; female and male feed young

Migration: non-migrator to partial; moves to find food

Food: fish, carrion, birds (mainly ducks)

Compare: The Turkey Vulture (pg. 47) is smaller, has two-toned wings and holds them in a V shape during flight unlike Bald Eagle, which holds its wings straight out.

Stan's Notes: Driven to near extinction due to DDT poisoning and illegal killing. Now making a comeback in North America. Returns to the same nest each year, adding more sticks and enlarging it to massive proportions, at times up to 1,000 pounds (450 kg). In the midair mating ritual, one eagle flips upside down and locks talons with another. Both tumble, then break apart to continue flight. Not uncommon for juvenile eagles to perform this mating ritual even though they have not reached breeding age. Thought to mate for life but will switch mates when not successful at reproducing. Juvenile attains the white head and tail at 4-5 years of age. Nests in the parks. Look for it around the larger lakes and rivers.

female
pg. 111

male

Lazuli Bunting
Passerina amoena

SUMMER

Size: 5½" (14 cm)

Male: A turquoise blue head, neck, back and tail. Cinnamon breast with cinnamon extending down the flanks slightly. White belly. Two bold white wing bars. Non-breeding male has a spotty blue head and back.

Female: overall grayish brown with a warm brown breast, light wash of blue on wings and tail, gray throat, light gray belly, two narrow white wing bars

Juvenile: similar to adult of the same sex

Nest: cup; female builds; 2-3 broods per year

Eggs: 3-5; pale blue without markings

Incubation: 11-13 days; female incubates

Fledging: 10-12 days; female and male feed young

Migration: complete, to Mexico

Food: insects, seeds; will visit seed feeders

Compare: The male Western Bluebird (pg. 91) is larger and darker blue with a darker brown breast. Male Mountain Bluebird (pg. 93) is all blue.

Stan's Notes: More common in lowland shrublands in Wyoming. Does not like dense forests. Strong association with water such as rivers and streams. Most active in June and July, when males sing from tall perches. After breeding, gathers in small flocks and tends to move up in elevations to hunt for insects and search for seeds. Populations have increased and range has expanded over the last 100 years.

Tree Swallow
Tachycineta bicolor

SUMMER

Size: 5-6" (13-15 cm)

Male: Blue green during spring and greener in fall. Appears to change color in direct sunlight. White chin, breast and belly. Long, pointed wing tips. Notched tail.

Female: similar to male, only duller

Juvenile: gray brown with a white belly and grayish breast band

Nest: cavity; female and male line old woodpecker cavity or nest box; 2 broods per year

Eggs: 4-6; white without markings

Incubation: 13-16 days; female incubates

Fledging: 20-24 days; female and male feed young

Migration: complete, to southwestern states, Mexico and Central America

Food: insects

Compare: Barn Swallow (pg. 89) has a rust belly and deeply forked tail. Western Bluebird (pg. 93) has a rusty red chest and lacks the white chin.

Stan's Notes: Most common at ponds and lakes during summer. Can be attracted to your yard with a nest box. Competes with bluebirds for cavities and nest boxes. Will travel great distances to find dropped feathers to line its grass nest. Occasionally seen playing, chasing after dropped feathers. Often seen flying back and forth across fields and water, feeding on insects. A good bird to have around because it eats many nuisance insects. Gathers in large flocks during migration. Common in both parks, especially around Yellowstone Lake.

Barn Swallow
Hirundo rustica

SUMMER

Size: 7" (18 cm)

Male: A sleek swallow. Blue black back, cinnamon belly and reddish brown chin. White spots on a long, deeply forked tail.

Female: same as male, but has a whiter chest

Juvenile: similar to adults, with a tan belly and chin and a shorter tail

Nest: cup; female and male construct; 2 broods per year

Eggs: 4-5; white with brown markings

Incubation: 13-17 days; female incubates

Fledging: 18-23 days; female and male feed young

Migration: complete, to Mexico, Central America and South America

Food: insects, prefers beetles, wasps and flies

Compare: Tree Swallow (pg. 87) has a white belly and chin and a notched tail. Larger than the Cliff Swallow (pg. 113) and Violet-green Swallow (pg. 279), which both lack the distinctive, deeply forked tail. The Violet-green Swallow is distinctively green with a white face.

Stan's Notes: Of the six swallow species in Wyoming, this is the only one that has a deeply forked tail. Unlike other swallows, Barn Swallows rarely glide in flight, so look for continuous flapping. Constructs a mud nest using up to 1,000 beak-loads of mud, often on barns, houses, under bridges or nearly any place that provides some shelter. Nests in colonies of 4-6 birds, but nesting alone is not uncommon. Drinks in flight, skimming water or getting water from wet leaves. Bathes while flying through rain or sprinklers.

male

female

Western Bluebird
Sialia mexicana

SUMMER

Size: 7" (18 cm)

Male: Deep blue head, neck, throat, back, wings and tail. Rusty red chest and flanks.

Female: similar to male, only duller with a gray head

Juvenile: similar to female, with a speckled chest

Nest: cavity, old woodpecker cavity, wooden nest box; female builds; 1-2 broods per year

Eggs: 4-6; pale blue without markings

Incubation: 13-14 days; female incubates

Fledging: 22-23 days; female and male feed young

Migration: complete, to southwestern states and Mexico

Food: insects, fruit

Compare: Mountain Bluebird (pg. 93) is similar, but it lacks the rusty red breast. Larger than male Lazuli Bunting (pg. 85), which has white wing bars.

Stan's Notes: Not as common as the Mountain Bluebird. Found in a variety of habitats, from agricultural land to clear-cuts. Requires a cavity for nesting. Competes with starlings for nest cavities. Like the Mountain Bluebird, it uses nest boxes, which are responsible for the stable populations. Populations dropped during the mid-1900s but recovered due to the efforts of concerned people who put up nest boxes, providing much-needed habitats for nesting. A courting male will fly in front of the female, spread his wings and tail, and perch next to her. Often goes in and out of its nest box or cavity as if to say, "Look inside." Male may offer food to the female to establish a pair bond. Look near Roosevelt Lodge and along the drive from Roosevelt to Yellowstone's Northeast Entrance.

male

female

Mountain Bluebird
Sialia currucoides

SUMMER

Size: 7" (18 cm)

Male: An overall sky-blue bird with a darker blue head, back, wings and tail and white lower belly. Thin black bill

Female: similar to male, but paler with a nearly gray head and chest and a whitish belly

Juvenile: similar to adult of the same sex

Nest: cavity, old woodpecker cavity, wooden nest box; female builds; 1-2 broods per year

Eggs: 4-6; pale blue without markings

Incubation: 13-14 days; female incubates

Fledging: 22-23 days; female and male feed young

Migration: complete, to southwestern states and Mexico

Food: insects, fruit

Compare: Similar to the Western Bluebird (pg. 91), but Mountain Bluebird is not as dark blue and lacks the rusty red chest.

Stan's Notes: Common in open mountainous country. Main diet is insects. Often hovers just before diving to the ground to grab an insect. Also hovers at the nest cavity entrance. Due to conservation of suitable nesting sites (dead trees with cavities and man-made nest boxes), populations have increased over the past 30 years. Like other bluebirds, Mountain Bluebirds take well to nest boxes and tolerate close contact with people. Female sits on baby birds (brood) for up to six days after the eggs hatch. Young imprint on their first nest box or cavity, then choose a similar type of box or cavity throughout their life. Any open field is a good place to look for Mountain Bluebirds. Search Mammoth Campground and along the shores of Yellowstone Lake at Mary Bay.

Pinyon Jay
Gymnorhinus cyanocephalus

YEAR-ROUND

Size: 11" (29 cm)

Male: A short-tailed dull blue jay. Head is darker blue than the rest of body. Faint white streaks on chin. Long, pointed black bill. Black legs.

Female: same as male

Juvenile: overall gray with blue highlights

Nest: cup; female and male construct; 1-2 broods per year

Eggs: 4-5; blue, green, gray or white with brown markings

Incubation: 16-17 days; female incubates

Fledging: 19-21 days; female and male feed young

Migration: non-migrator

Food: seeds, insects, fruit; will visit feeders

Compare: The Steller's Jay (pg. 97) has a black head and crest. The Canada Jay (pg. 249) is gray with a mostly white head.

Stan's Notes: This is a highly specialized jay, usually seen near pine trees. Gathers nuts from cones, storing them in large caches, often on the ground. An important seed disperser, with forgotten caches sprouting into new trees. Can breed in late winter in years with abundant seed production. Gregarious, it breeds in colonies of up to 50 pairs. Starts to breed at age 3. Mates are often the same age and stay together for years. During winter, flocks of up to several hundred gather to roost and find food, and move on when supplies are low. Sings a soft flight song, "hoyi-hoyi-hoyi-hoyi." Often walks rather than hops, like most other jays. Closely related to Clark's Nutcracker.

Steller's Jay
Cyanocitta stelleri

YEAR-ROUND

Size: 11" (28 cm)

Male: Dark blue wings, tail and belly. Black head, nape of neck and chest. Large, pointed black crest on the head that can be lifted at will. Distinctive white streaks on forehead and just above eyes.

Female: same as male

Juvenile: similar to adult, lacks white markings on the forehead and the white eye stripe

Nest: cup; female and male build; 1 brood per year

Eggs: 3-5; pale green with brown markings

Incubation: 14-16 days; female incubates

Fledging: 16-18 days; female and male feed young

Migration: non-migrator

Food: insects, berries, seeds; will visit seed feeders

Compare: The Pinyon Jay (pg. 95) is the same size, but lacks the black head and crest. The Canada Jay (pg. 249) lacks any blue and a crest.

Stan's Notes: Common resident of foothills and lower mountains from 6,000-8,000 feet (1,850-2,450 m). Usually seen in coniferous forests. Rarely competes with Canada Jays, which occupy higher elevations. Thought to mate for life. Rarely disperses very far, often breeding within 10 miles (16 km) of birthplace. Several subspecies are found throughout the Rocky Mountains. Other varieties lack the white markings. Named after Arctic explorer Georg W. Steller, who discovered the bird on the coast of Alaska in 1741. Check any of the campgrounds in both parks that have a healthy stand of conifers. Also search pull-offs at mid-level elevations.

male

female

Belted Kingfisher
Megaceryle alcyon

YEAR-ROUND

Size: 13" (33 cm)

Male: Large blue bird with a white belly. Broad blue gray breast band. Ragged crest that is raised and lowered at will. Large head with a long, thick black bill. Small white spot directly in front of red brown eyes. Black wing tips with splashes of white that flash during flight.

Female: same as male, but a rusty breast band in addition to the blue gray band, and rusty flanks

Juvenile: similar to female

Nest: cavity; female and male excavate; 1 brood per year

Eggs: 6-7; white without markings

Incubation: 23-24 days; female and male incubate

Fledging: 23-24 days; female and male feed young

Migration: non-migrator to partial in Wyoming; moves around to find open water

Food: small fish

Compare: Larger than the Steller's Jay (pg. 97), which has a black head and more prominent crest. Clark's Nutcracker (pg. 253) and Canada Jay (pg. 249) lack the breast band of Kingfisher.

Stan's Notes: Perching on a branch near water, this bird will dive headfirst for small fish and return to the branch to feed. Gives a loud machine-gun-like call. Mates recognize each other by their calls. Digs a deep nest cavity in the bank of a river or lake. Parents drop dead fish into water, teaching the young to dive. Regurgitates bone pellets after meals. Check any water in both parks. Look in the vicinity of the 45th Parallel Bridge.

Chipping Sparrow
Spizella passerina

SUMMER

Size: 5" (13 cm)

Male: Small gray brown sparrow with a clear gray breast, rusty crown and white eyebrows. A black eye line and thin gray black bill. Two faint wing bars.

Female: same as male

Juvenile: similar to adult, has a streaked breast, lacks the rusty crown

Nest: cup; female builds; 2 broods per year

Eggs: 3-5; blue green with brown markings

Incubation: 11-14 days; female incubates

Fledging: 10-12 days; female and male feed young

Migration: complete, to southwestern states, Mexico and Central America

Food: insects, seeds; will come to ground feeders

Compare: The Lark Sparrow (pg. 123) is larger and has a white chest and central spot. Song Sparrow (pg. 115) has a heavily streaked chest. The female House Finch (pg. 105) also has a streaked chest.

Stan's Notes: A common garden or yard bird, often seen feeding on dropped seeds beneath feeders. Gathers in large family groups to feed in preparation for migration. Migrates at night in flocks of 20-30 birds. The common name comes from the male's fast "chip" call. Often just called Chippy. Builds nest low in dense shrubs and almost always lines it with animal hair. Common cowbird host. Can be very unafraid of people, allowing you to approach closely before it flies away.

Pine Siskin
Spinus pinus

YEAR-ROUND
WINTER

Size: 5" (13 cm)

Male: Small brown finch. A heavily streaked back, breast and belly. Yellow wing bars. Yellow at base of tail. Thin bill.

Female: similar to male, with less yellow

Juvenile: similar to adult, light yellow tinge over the breast and chin

Nest: modified cup; female builds; 2 broods

Eggs: 3-4; greenish blue with brown markings

Incubation: 12-13 days; female incubates

Fledging: 14-15 days; female and male feed young

Migration: non-migrator to irruptive; moves around the U.S. in search of food

Food: seeds, insects; will come to seed feeders

Compare: Female American Goldfinch (pg. 317) lacks streaks and has white wing bars. The female House Finch (pg. 105) has a streaked chest, but it lacks yellow wing bars.

Stan's Notes: Often considered a winter finch, it's also a nesting resident in portions of Wyoming. Conspicuous in some winters, absent in others. Seen in flocks of up to 20 birds, often with other species of finches. Gathers in flocks and moves around, visiting feeders. Comes to thistle feeders. Breeds in small groups. Male feeds the female during incubation. Juveniles lose the yellow tint by late summer of their first year. Builds nest toward the end of coniferous branches, where needles are dense, helping to conceal. Nests are often only a few feet apart.

male
pg. 297

female

House Finch
Haemorhous mexicanus

YEAR-ROUND

Size: 5" (13 cm)

Female: A plain brown bird with a heavily streaked white chest.

Male: orange red face, chest and rump, brown cap, brown marking behind eyes, brown wings streaked with white, a streaked belly

Juvenile: similar to female

Nest: cup, occasionally in a cavity, female builds; 2 broods per year

Eggs: 4-5; pale blue, lightly marked

Incubation: 12-14 days; female incubates

Fledging: 15-19 days; female and male feed young

Migration: non-migrator to partial; will move around to find food

Food: seeds, fruit, leaf buds; will visit seed feeders

Compare: Female American Goldfinch (pg. 317) has a clear breast and white wing bars. Similar to the Pine Siskin (pg. 103), but lacks the yellow wing bars and has a much larger bill.

Stan's Notes: Very social, visiting feeders in small flocks. Can be the most common bird at feeders. Likes to nest in hanging flower baskets. Male sings a loud, cheerful warbling song. Historically it occurred from the Pacific Coast to the Rocky Mountains, with a few reaching the eastern side. Birds introduced to Long Island, New York, in the 1940s have populated the entire eastern U.S. Now found throughout the U.S. Male feeds the incubating female. Suffers from a fatal eye disease that causes the eyes to crust.

House Wren
Troglodytes aedon

SUMMER

Size: 5" (13 cm)

Male: A small all-brown bird with lighter brown markings on tail and wings. Slightly curved brown bill. Often holds its tail erect.

Female: same as male

Juvenile: same as adult

Nest: cavity; female and male line just about any nest cavity; 2 broods per year

Eggs: 4-6; tan with brown markings

Incubation: 10-13 days; female and male incubate

Fledging: 12-15 days; female and male feed young

Migration: complete, to southwestern states and Mexico

Food: insects, spiders, snails

Compare: The long curved bill and long upturned tail differentiates the House Wren from sparrows.

Stan's Notes: A prolific songster, it will sing from dawn until dusk during the mating season. Easily attracted to nest boxes. In spring, the male chooses several prospective nesting cavities and places a few small twigs in each. Female inspects each, chooses one, and finishes the nest building. She will completely fill the nest cavity with uniformly small twigs, then line a small depression at the back of the cavity with pine needles and grass. Often has trouble fitting long twigs through the nest cavity hole. Tries many different directions and approaches until successful. Look for this bird in lower elevations with dead trees, where woodpeckers have made their homes.

male pg. 227

female

pink-sided

Oregon female

Dark-eyed Junco
Junco hyemalis

YEAR-ROUND
WINTER

Size: 5½" (14 cm)

Female: Round, dark-eyed bird with a tan-to-brown chest, head and back. White belly. Ivory-to-pink bill. Since the outermost tail feathers are white, tail appears as a white V in flight.

Male: same as female, only slate gray to charcoal

Juvenile: similar to female, but streaked chest and head

Nest: cup; female and male construct; 2 broods per year

Eggs: 3-5; white with reddish brown markings

Incubation: 12-13 days; female incubates

Fledging: 10-13 days; male and female feed young

Migration: complete to non-migrator in Wyoming

Food: seeds, insects; will come to seed feeders

Compare: Rarely confused with any other bird. Small flocks feed under bird feeders in winter.

Stan's Notes: A year-round bird in Wyoming in higher elevations but usually more commonly seen in winter. Migrates from Canada to Wyoming and beyond. Females tend to fly farther south than the males. Spends the winter in the foothills and plains after snow-melt. Builds nest in a variety of wooded habitats. Adheres to a rigid social hierarchy, with dominant birds chasing the less dominant. Its white outer tail feathers flash when in flight. Often seen in small flocks on the ground, where it will "double-scratch" with both feet simultaneously to expose seeds and insects. Eats many weed seeds. Several junco species were combined into one, simply called Dark-eyed Junco (see lower insets). Pink-sided and Oregon females look nearly identical and are hard to differentiate. Look for all varieties at any time of year in both parks.

male
pg. 85

female

Lazuli Bunting
Passerina amoena

SUMMER

Size: 5½" (14 cm)

Female: Overall grayish brown with a warm brown breast, light wash of blue on wings and tail, gray throat and light gray belly. Two narrow white wing bars.

Male: turquoise blue head, neck, back and tail, cinnamon breast, white belly, two bold white wing bars

Juvenile: similar to adult of the same sex

Nest: cup; female builds; 2-3 broods per year

Eggs: 3-5; pale blue without markings

Incubation: 11-13 days; female incubates

Fledging: 10-12 days; female and male feed young

Migration: complete, to Mexico

Food: insects, seeds; will visit seed feeders

Compare: The female Western Bluebird (pg. 91) and Mountain Bluebird (pg. 93) are larger and have much more blue than the female Lazuli.

Stan's Notes: More common in lowland shrublands in Wyoming. Does not like dense forests. Strong association with water such as rivers and streams. Most active in June and July, when males sing from tall perches. After breeding, gathers in small flocks and tends to move up in elevations to hunt for insects and search for seeds. Populations have increased and range has expanded over the last 100 years.

Cliff Swallow

Petrochelidon pyrrhonota

SUMMER

Size: 5½" (14 cm)

Male: A uniquely patterned swallow with a dark back, wings and cap. Distinctive tan-to-rust rump, cheeks and forehead.

Female: same as male

Juvenile: similar to adult, lacks distinct patterning

Nest: gourd-shaped, made of mud; male and female build; 1-2 broods per year

Eggs: 4-6; pale white with brown markings

Incubation: 14-16 days; male and female incubate

Fledging: 21-24 days; female and male feed young

Migration: complete, to South America

Food: insects

Compare: Smaller than Barn Swallow (pg. 89), which has a distinctive, deeply forked tail and blue back and wings. Tree Swallow (pg. 87) lacks tan-to-rust coloring. Violet-green Swallow (pg. 279) is green with a bright white face.

Stan's Notes: Common and widespread in Wyoming in summer. Common around bridges (especially bridges over water) and rural housing (especially in open country near cliffs). Builds a gourd-shaped nest with a funnel-like entrance pointing down. A colony nester, with many nests lined up beneath building eaves or cliff overhangs. Will carry balls of mud up to a mile to construct its nest. Many in the colony return to the same nest site each year. Not unusual to have two broods per season. If the number of nests underneath eaves becomes a problem, wait until the young have left the nests to hose off the mud. Look at Wildlife Overlook at Trout Creek or the backside of Soda Butte for these birds.

Song Sparrow
Melospiza melodia

YEAR-ROUND

Size: 5-6" (13-15 cm)

Male: A common brown sparrow with heavy dark streaks on the breast coalescing into a central dark spot.

Female: same as male

Juvenile: similar to adult, finely streaked breast, lacks a central spot

Nest: cup; female builds; 2 broods per year

Eggs: 3-4; pale blue to green, marked with reddish brown splotches

Incubation: 12-14 days; female incubates

Fledging: 9-12 days; female and male feed young

Migration: partial to non-migrator in Wyoming

Food: insects, seeds; rarely visits seed feeders

Compare: Similar to other brown sparrows. Look for the heavily streaked breast with a central dark spot to help identify the Song Sparrow.

Stan's Notes: Many subspecies or varieties of Song Sparrow, but the dark central spot is seen in each variant. Defends a small territory by singing from thick shrubs. This is a constant songster that repeats its loud, clear song every couple minutes. Song varies in structure, but it is basically the same from region to region. A ground feeder, look for it to scratch at the same time with both feet, or "double-scratch," to expose seeds. While the female builds another nest for a second brood, the male often takes over feeding the young. Unlike many other sparrow species, Song Sparrows will rarely flock together. A common host of the Brown-headed Cowbird.

male

female

House Sparrow
Passer domesticus

YEAR-ROUND

Size: 6" (15 cm)

Male: Medium sparrow-like bird. Large black spot on the throat extending down to the breast. Brown back. One white wing bar. Gray belly and crown.

Female: slightly smaller than the male, light brown, lacks the throat patch and the wing bar

Juvenile: similar to female

Nest: domed cup nest, within a cavity; female and male build; 2-3 broods per year

Eggs: 4-6; white with brown markings

Incubation: 10-12 days; female incubates

Fledging: 14-17 days; female and male feed young

Migration: non-migrator; moves around to find food

Food: seeds, insects, fruit; comes to seed feeders

Compare: Lacks the rusty crown of Chipping Sparrow (pg. 101). Look for the black bib of the male House Sparrow. Female House Sparrow has a clear breast and lacks a cap.

Stan's Notes: One of the first bird songs heard in cities in spring. A familiar city bird, nearly always in small flocks. Also found on farms. Introduced from Europe to Central Park, New York, in 1850, it is now found throughout North America. Related to Old World sparrows; not related to any sparrows in the United States. Constructs an oversized domed nest with scraps of plastic, paper, dried grass and whatever else is available. An aggressive bird that will kill the young of other birds in order to take over a cavity.

male

female

Chestnut-collared Longspur
Calcarius ornatus

MIGRATION
SUMMER

Size: 6" (15 cm)

Male: Overall brown with black and white stripes on the head. Rusty red nape "collar." Yellow chin and throat. Black chest and belly. Small pointed bill. Dramatic color change during winter, similar to female.

Female: duller brown than male, lacks a black chest, belly and stripes on head and a red nape

Juvenile: similar to female, but duller

Nest: cup; female builds; 1-2 broods per year

Eggs: 3-6; white with brown markings

Incubation: 10-13 days; female incubates

Fledging: 9-14 days; male and female feed young

Migration: complete, to Texas and Mexico

Food: insects, seeds

Compare: The male's rusty red nape and black chest and belly easily help identify this grassland bird. The female resembles a sparrow; look for the dark wing spots.

Stan's Notes: One of four longspur species in North America. This bird is found in grasslands and native prairies throughout eastern Wyoming. Common name "Longspur" refers to the long rear toe and nail, which are nearly twice the length of the front two toes. Nest is well concealed in a shallow depression under dense vegetation on the ground, with the rim flush with the ground. Male performs a mating flight with rapid wing beats and a soft song. Adults eat insects and seeds. Young are fed an insect diet. Breeding plumage seen from March to September.

female

male
pg. 53

non-breeding
male

Lark Bunting
Calamospiza melanocorys

MIGRATION
SUMMER

Size: 6½" (16 cm)

Female: Brown bird with a heavily streaked breast and white belly. Black vertical line on each side of a white chin. May have a central dark spot on the breast. Faint white eyebrows.

Male: black bird with a large broad head, white wing patches and large bluish gray bill

Juvenile: similar to adult of the same sex

Nest: cup; female builds; 1-2 broods per year

Eggs: 4-6; pale blue with markings

Incubation: 11-13 days; female and male incubate

Fledging: 8-12 days; female and male feed young

Migration: complete, to southwestern states and Mexico

Food: insects, seeds

Compare: Appears similar to open country sparrows. The female Red-winged Blackbird (pg. 141) lacks the white belly and chin.

Stan's Notes: Common in the dry plains and sagebrush regions of Wyoming. Male flashes white wing patches on his short, rounded wings while flying with shallow wing beats. Male takes to the air to display to the female, setting his wings in a V position and floating back, rocking like a butterfly, singing a most amazing song. Song is like that of Old World larks, hence the common name. Will flock in autumn with hundreds, if not thousands, of other Lark Buntings for migration.

Lark Sparrow
Chondestes grammacus

SUMMER

Size: 6½" (16 cm)

Male: Brown bird with a unique rusty red, white and black pattern on head. White breast with a central black spot. Gray rump and white edges on a gray tail, as seen in flight.

Female: same as male

Juvenile: similar to adult, no rusty red on head

Nest: cup, on the ground; female builds; 1 brood per year

Eggs: 3-6; pale white with brown markings

Incubation: 10-12 days; male and female incubate

Fledging: 10-12 days; female and male feed young

Migration: complete, to coastal Mexico and Central America

Food: seeds, insects

Compare: The White-crowned Sparrow (pg. 125) lacks the Lark Sparrow's rusty red pattern on the head and central spot on a white chest. Larger than Chipping Sparrow (pg. 101), which has a similar rusty color on the head, but it lacks Lark's white chest and central spot.

Stan's Notes: This is a large and handsome sparrow, usually seen on the ground. One of the best songsters. Also well known for its courtship strutting, chasing and lark-like flight pattern (rapid wing beats with tail spread). A bird of open fields, pastures and prairies, found almost anywhere there are no mountains. Very common during migration, when large flocks congregate. Uses the same nest for several years if the first brood is successful.

juvenile

White-crowned Sparrow
Zonotrichia leucophrys

MIGRATION
SUMMER

Size: 6½-7½" (16-19 cm)

Male: A brown sparrow with a gray breast and a black-and-white striped crown. Small, thin pink bill.

Female: same as male

Juvenile: similar to adult, with brown stripes on the head instead of white

Nest: cup; female builds; 2 broods per year

Eggs: 3-5; color varies from greenish to bluish to whitish with red brown markings

Incubation: 11-14 days; female incubates

Fledging: 8-12 days; male and female feed young

Migration: complete, to southwestern states and Mexico

Food: insects, seeds, berries; visits ground feeders

Compare: The Lark Sparrow (pg. 123) has a rusty red pattern on its head and central black spot on a white chest. Female Lark Bunting (pg. 121) lacks a black-and-white striped crown. Song Sparrow (pg. 115) has heavy dark streaks on its chest coalescing into a central spot.

Stan's Notes: A prolific songster. Usually in groups of as many as 20 birds during migration, when it can be seen feeding underneath seed feeders. Males arrive on the breeding grounds before females and establish territories by singing from perches. A ground feeder, scratching backward with both feet at the same time. Male takes most of the responsibility to raise the young while female starts the second brood. Only 9-12 days separate broods. Nests in Wyoming, Canada and Alaska.

Fox Sparrow
Passerella iliaca

MIGRATION
SUMMER

Size: 7" (18 cm)

Male: Plump brown sparrow with a gray head, back and rump. White chest and belly with rusty brown streaks. Rusty tail and wings.

Female: same as male

Juvenile: same as adult

Nest: cup; female builds; 2 broods per year

Eggs: 2-4; pale green with reddish markings

Incubation: 12-14 days; female incubates

Fledging: 10-11 days; female and male feed young

Migration: complete, to southwestern states

Food: seeds, insects; comes to feeders

Compare: The male Spotted Towhee (pg. 29) is found in a similar habitat, but it has a black head.

Stan's Notes: One of the largest sparrows. Several color variations, depending upon the part of the country. Usually seen alone or in small groups. Often beneath seed feeders, looking for seeds and insects. Scratches like a chicken with both feet at the same time to find food. Builds nest on the ground in brush and along forest edges. The common name "Sparrow" comes from the Anglo-Saxon word *spearwa*, meaning "flutterer," as applied to any small bird. "Fox" refers to its rusty coloring.

Horned Lark
Eremophila alpestris

YEAR-ROUND

Size: 7-8" (18-20 cm)

Male: A sleek tan-to-brown bird. Black necklace with a yellow chin and black bill. Two tiny "horns" on the top of head; can be difficult to see. A dark tail with white outer feathers, noticeable in flight.

Female: duller than male, "horns" less noticeable

Juvenile: lacks the black markings and yellow chin, doesn't form "horns" until second year

Nest: ground; female builds; 2-3 broods per year

Eggs: 3-4; gray with brown markings

Incubation: 11-12 days; female incubates

Fledging: 9-12 days; female and male feed young

Migration: non-migrator to partial in Wyoming

Food: seeds, insects

Compare: Smaller than Western Meadowlark (pg. 339), which shares the black necklace and yellow chin. Look for black marks in front of the eyes to help identify the Horned Lark.

Stan's Notes: The only true lark native to North America. Moves around during winter to find food. Horned Larks are birds of open ground. Common in rural areas, frequently seen in large flocks. Population increased in North America over the past century due to the clearing of land for farming. Can have up to three broods per year because the birds get such an early start. Male performs a fluttering courtship flight high in the air while singing a high-pitched song. Female performs a fluttering distraction display if the nest is disturbed. Can renest about a week after the brood fledges. "Lark" comes from the Middle English word *laverock*, or "a lark."

male pg. 25

female

Brown-headed Cowbird
Molothrus ater

SUMMER

Size: 7½" (19 cm)

Female: Dull brown bird with no obvious markings. Pointed, sharp gray bill. Dark eyes.

Male: glossy black bird, chocolate brown head

Juvenile: similar to female, but dull gray color and has a streaked chest

Nest: no nest; lays eggs in the nests of other birds

Eggs: 5-7; white with brown markings

Incubation: 10-13 days; host bird incubates eggs

Fledging: 10-11 days; host birds feed young

Migration: complete, to southwestern states

Food: insects, seeds; will come to seed feeders

Compare: The female Red-winged Blackbird (pg. 141) is slightly larger and has white eyebrows and a streaked chest. European Starling (pg. 27) is the same size as Brown-headed Cowbird, but it has speckles and a shorter tail.

Stan's Notes: A blackbird family member. Of about 750 species of parasitic birds worldwide, this is the only parasitic bird in the state, laying eggs in host birds' nests, leaving others to raise its young. Cowbirds are known to have laid eggs in the nests of over 200 species of birds. Some birds reject cowbird eggs, but most will incubate them and raise the young, even to the exclusion of their own. Look for warblers and other birds feeding young birds twice their own size. Flocks of cowbirds follow herds of bison in both parks; look for them landing on the backs of bison and other large animals. Seen in busier parts of Yellowstone, such as Old Faithful.

1 year old

Bohemian Waxwing

Cedar Waxwing
Bombycilla cedrorum

YEAR-ROUND

Size: 7½" (19 cm)

Male: Very sleek-looking gray-to-brown bird with a pointed crest, light yellow belly and bandit-like black mask. Tip of tail is bright yellow. Red wing tips look like they were dipped in red wax.

Female: same as male

Juvenile: grayish with a heavily streaked chest, lacks red wing tips, black mask and sleek look

Nest: cup; female and male construct; 1 brood per year, occasionally 2

Eggs: 4-6; pale blue with brown markings

Incubation: 10-12 days; female incubates

Fledging: 14-18 days; female and male feed young

Migration: non-migrator to partial; moves around during winter in search of food

Food: cedar cones, fruit, insects

Compare: Cedar Waxwing's larger, less common cousin, Bohemian Waxwing (see inset), has white on its wings and rust under its tail.

Stan's Notes: The name is derived from its red wax-like wing tips and preference for the small, blueberry-like cones of the cedar. Mostly seen in flocks, moving around from area to area, looking for berries. Feeds on insects during summer, before berries are abundant. Wanders during winter to find available food supplies. Spends most of its time at the top of tall trees. Listen for the high-pitched "sreee" whistling sounds it constantly makes. Obtains its mask after the first year and red wing tips after the second. Look in the trees near Albright Visitor Center for waxwings.

winter

breeding

Spotted Sandpiper
Actitis macularius

SUMMER

Size: 8" (20 cm)

Male: Olive brown back. Long bill and long, dull yellow legs. White line over the eyes. Breeding plumage has black spots on a white chest and belly. Winter has a clear chest and belly.

Female: same as male

Juvenile: similar to winter adult, with a darker bill

Nest: ground; male builds; 2 broods per year

Eggs: 3-4; brownish with brown markings

Incubation: 20-24 days; male incubates

Fledging: 17-21 days; male feeds young

Migration: complete, to southwestern states, Mexico and Central and South America

Food: aquatic insects

Compare: Killdeer (pg. 151) has two black neck bands. Look for the Spotted Sandpiper to bob its tail up and down while standing. Look for breeding Spotted Sandpiper's black spots extending from the chest to the belly.

Stan's Notes: One of the few shorebirds that will dive underwater when pursued. Can fly straight up out of the water. Holds wings in a cup-like arc during flight, rarely lifting them above a horizontal plane. Constantly bobs its tail while standing. Walks as if delicately balanced. Female mates with multiple males and lays eggs in up to five nests. Male incubates and cares for the young. Winter plumage Spotted Sandpipers lack black spots on the chest and belly. Look for them along the shores of large lakes in both parks.

male
pg. 295

female

Black-headed Grosbeak

Pheucticus melanocephalus

SUMMER

Size: 8" (20 cm)

Female: Appears like an overgrown sparrow. Overall brown with a lighter breast and belly. Large two-toned bill. Prominent white eyebrows. Yellow wing linings, as seen in flight.

Male: burnt orange breast, neck and rump, black head, tail and wings with irregular-shaped white wing patches, large bill with upper bill darker than the lower

Juvenile: similar to adult of the same sex

Nest: cup; female builds; 1 brood per year

Eggs: 3-4; pale green or bluish with brown marks

Incubation: 11-13 days; female and male incubate

Fledging: 11-13 days; female and male feed young

Migration: complete, to Mexico, Central America and northern South America

Food: seeds, insects, fruit; comes to seed feeders

Compare: Female House Finch (pg. 105) is smaller, has more streaking on the chest and bill isn't as large. Look for the unusual bicolored bill of the female Black-headed Grosbeak.

Stan's Notes: A bird that nests in a wide variety of habitats, but seems to prefer the foothills slightly more than other places. Both males and females sing and aggressively defend their nests against intruders. Song is very similar to the American Robin's and Western Tanager's, making it hard to tell them apart by song. Populations are increasing in Wyoming and across the U.S.

male
pg. 29

female

Spotted Towhee
Pipilo maculatus

SUMMER

Size: 8½" (22 cm)

Female: Brown head, dirty red-brown sides and white belly. Multiple white spots on the wings and sides. Long black tail with a white tip. Rich red eyes.

Male: mostly black, lacks a brown head

Juvenile: brown with a heavily streaked chest

Nest: cup; female builds; 1-2 broods per year

Eggs: 3-5; white with brown markings

Incubation: 12-14 days; female and male incubate

Fledging: 10-12 days; female and male feed young

Migration: complete, to southwestern states

Food: seeds, fruit, insects; will visit feeders

Compare: Smaller than the American Robin (pg. 247).

Stan's Notes: Less common than Green-tailed Towhee but lives in a similar habitat. Inhabits a variety of habitats, from thick brush and forests to suburban backyards. Often scratches noisily through dead leaves on the ground for food; more than 70 percent of its diet is plant material. Eats more insects during spring and summer. Well known for retreating from danger by walking away rather than taking to flight. Cup nest is nearly always on the ground under bushes but away from where the male perches to sing. Begins breeding in April. Lays eggs in May. After breeding season, moves to higher elevations. Song and plumage vary geographically.

male
pg. 31

female

Red-winged Blackbird
Agelaius phoeniceus

YEAR-ROUND
SUMMER

Size: 8½" (22 cm)

Female: Heavily streaked brown bird with a pointed brown bill and white eyebrows.

Male: jet-black bird with red and yellow patches on upper wings, pointed black bill

Juvenile: same as female

Nest: cup; female builds; 2-3 broods per year

Eggs: 3-4; bluish green with brown markings

Incubation: 10-12 days; female incubates

Fledging: 11-14 days; female and male feed young

Migration: complete to non-migrator in Wyoming

Food: seeds, insects; will come to seed feeders

Compare: Larger than female Brown-headed Cowbird (pg. 131), and smaller than female Yellow-headed Blackbird (pg. 147) and female Brewer's Blackbird (pg. 145). All three lack white eyebrows and streaks on the chest.

Stan's Notes: It's a sure sign of spring when the Red-wings return to the marshes. Flocks with as many as 10,000 birds have been reported. Males arrive before females and defend their territories by singing from the top of surrounding vegetation. Male repeats his call from cattail tops while showing off his red and yellow shoulder patches. Female chooses a mate and often nests over shallow water in thick stands of cattails. Can be aggressive when defending the nest. Feeds mostly on seeds during fall and spring, switching to insects in summer.

male

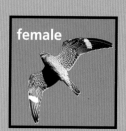

female

Common Nighthawk
Chordeiles minor

SUMMER

Size: 9" (22.5 cm)

Male: Camouflaged brown and white bird with a white chin. A distinctive white band across the wings and tail, seen only in flight.

Female: similar to male, but with a tan chin, lacks a white tail band

Juvenile: similar to female

Nest: no nest; lays eggs on the ground, usually on rocks or a rooftop; 1 brood per year

Eggs: 2; cream with lavender markings

Incubation: 19-20 days; female and male incubate

Fledging: 20-21 days; female and male feed young

Migration: complete, to South America

Food: insects caught in air

Compare: Look for the obvious white wing band of the Nighthawk in flight, and the characteristic flap-flap-flap-glide pattern.

Stan's Notes: Usually only seen flying at dusk or after sunset, but it is not uncommon for it to be seen sitting on a branch, sleeping during the day. Very noisy bird, repeating a "peenting" call during flight. Alternates slow wing beats with bursts of quick wing beats. A prolific insect eater. Prefers gravel rooftops for nesting in cities, but these populations are decreasing as flat-topped roofs covered in gravel are converted to regular roofs. Nests on the ground in the country. The male's distinctive mating ritual in spring is a steep diving flight ending with a loud popping noise. One of the first birds to migrate in autumn. Seen in large flocks, all heading south.

male pg. 33

female

Brewer's Blackbird
Euphagus cyanocephalus

SUMMER

Size: 9" (22.5 cm)

Female: An overall grayish brown bird. Legs and bill are nearly black. Most have dark eyes; some have bright white or pale yellow eyes.

Male: glossy black, shining green in direct sunlight, head is purplish, eyes white or pale yellow

Juvenile: similar to female

Nest: cup; female builds; 1-2 broods per year

Eggs: 4-6; gray with brown markings

Incubation: 12-14 days; female incubates

Fledging: 13-14 days; female and male feed young

Migration: complete, to southwestern states

Food: insects, seeds, fruit

Compare: Larger in size and darker in color than the female Brown-headed Cowbird (pg. 131). Female Red-winged Blackbird (pg. 141) is similar in size, but it has a heavily streaked chest and prominent white eyebrows.

Stan's Notes: Often in fields and open places such as wet pastures and mountain meadows up to 10,000 feet (3,050 m). Males and some females are easily identified by their bright, nearly white eyes. A cowbird host. Usually nests in a shrub, small tree or on ground. Prefers to nest in small colonies of up to 20 pairs. Doesn't get along with Common Grackles; often driven out of the nest area by the expansion of grackles. Gathers in large flocks to migrate with Brown-headed Cowbirds, Red-winged Blackbirds and other blackbirds. Expanding its range in North America.

male pg. 35

female

Yellow-headed Blackbird
Xanthocephalus xanthocephalus

SUMMER

Size: 9-11" (22.5-28 cm)

Female: Large brown bird with a dull yellow head and chest. Slightly smaller than the male.

Male: black bird with a lemon yellow head, breast and nape of neck, black mask, gray bill and white wing patches

Juvenile: similar to female

Nest: cup; female builds; 2 broods per year

Eggs: 3-5; greenish white with brown markings

Incubation: 11-13 days; female incubates

Fledging: 9-12 days; female feeds young

Migration: complete, to southwestern states and Mexico

Food: insects, seeds; will come to ground feeders

Compare: Larger than the female Red-winged Blackbird (pg. 141), which has white eyebrows and a streaked chest.

Stan's Notes: Usually heard before seen; the call is low, hoarse, raspy or metallic-sounding. Nests in deep water marshes unlike its cousin, the Red-winged Blackbird, which prefers shallow water. The male gives an impressive mating display, flying with his head drooped and feet and tail pointing down while steadily beating his wings. Female incubates alone and feeds 3-5 young. Young keep low and out of sight for up to three weeks before starting to fly. Migrates in flocks of up to 200 with other blackbirds. Flocks made up mainly of males return first in early April; females return later. Most colonies consist of 20-100 nests. Nests in lower elevations, such as in the ponds of Junction Butte, east of Yellowstone Bridge.

in flight

male

juvenile

female

in flight
juvenile

American Kestrel
Falco sparverius

YEAR-ROUND

Size:	9-11" (22.5-28 cm); up to 2-foot wingspan
Male:	Rusty brown back and tail. White breast with dark spots. Two vertical black lines on a white face. Blue gray wings. Distinctive wide black band with a white edge on tip of a rusty tail.
Female:	similar to male, but slightly larger, has rusty brown wings and dark bands on tail
Juvenile:	same as adult of the same sex
Nest:	cavity; doesn't build a nest within; 1 brood
Eggs:	4-5; white with brown markings
Incubation:	29-31 days; male and female incubate
Fledging:	30-31 days; female and male feed young
Migration:	partial to non-migrator in Wyoming
Food:	insects, small mammals and birds, reptiles
Compare:	Prairie Falcon (pg. 175) is larger and has dark armpits. Look for two vertical black stripes on the American Kestrel's face. No other small bird of prey has a rusty back and tail.

Stan's Notes: A falcon that was once called Sparrow Hawk due to its small size. Could be called Grasshopper Hawk because it eats many grasshoppers. Can see ultraviolet light; this helps it locate mice and other small mammals by their urine, which glows bright yellow in ultraviolet light. Hovers near roads, then dives for prey. Adapts quickly to a wooden nest box. Has pointed, swept-back wings, seen in flight. Perches nearly upright. An unusual raptor in that males and females have quite different markings. Watch them pump their tails up and down after landing on perches. Anywhere along Lamar Valley is a good place to see kestrels in all seasons.

Killderr

Killdeer
Charadrius vociferus

SUMMER

Size: 11" (28 cm)

Male: An upland shorebird with two black bands around the neck like a necklace. Brown back and white belly. Bright reddish orange rump, visible in flight.

Female: same as male

Juvenile: similar to adult, with a single neck band

Nest: ground; male builds; 2 broods per year

Eggs: 3-5; tan with brown markings

Incubation: 24-28 days; male and female incubate

Fledging: 25 days; male and female lead their young to food

Migration: complete, southwestern states, Mexico and Central America

Food: insects

Compare: The Spotted Sandpiper (pg. 135) is found around water and lacks the two neck bands of the Killdeer.

Stan's Notes: The only shorebird with two black neck bands. It is known for its broken wing impression, which draws intruders away from the nest. Once clear of the nest, the Killdeer takes flight. Nests are just a slight depression in a gravel area, often very hard to see. Young look like miniature adults on stilts when first hatched. They are able to follow their parents and peck for insects soon after birth. Technically classified as a shorebird but doesn't live at the shore. Often seen in vacant fields or by railroads. Migrates in small flocks. Gives a very distinctive "kill-deer" call.

151

Upland Sandpiper
Bartramia longicauda

MIGRATION
SUMMER

Size: 12" (30 cm)

Male: Overall brown shorebird. Long yellow legs, a short, brown-tipped yellow bill and a white belly. Appears to have a thin neck and small head in relationship to its body.

Female: same as male

Juvenile: similar to adult

Nest: ground; female and male construct; 1 brood per year

Eggs: 3-4; off-white with red markings

Incubation: 21-27 days; female and male incubate

Fledging: 30-31 days; female and male feed young

Migration: complete, to South America

Food: insects, seeds

Compare: The breeding Spotted Sandpiper (pg. 135) is smaller, has shorter legs, black spots on a white breast, and is seen in very different habitats; Spotted is almost always near water while the Upland is found in grassy meadows and prairies.

Stan's Notes: An aptly named shorebird of dry grasslands. Often seen standing on fence posts or other perches in prairie or grassland habitats. Often found in prairies and grasslands that were burned, where foraging for food is easier. A true indicator of high-quality habitat, this shorebird returns to a more watery habitat after breeding and just before migrating. Frequently holds its wings open over its back for several seconds just after landing. Formerly known as Upland Plover. Was hunted in the late 1800s.

red-shafted
male

yellow-shafted
male

yellow-shafted
female

red-shafted
female

Northern Flicker
Colaptes auratus

YEAR-ROUND

Size: 12" (30 cm)

Male: Brown and black woodpecker with a large white rump patch, visible only when flying. Black necklace above a speckled breast. Gray head with a brown cap. Red mustache.

Female: same as male, but lacks a red mustache

Juvenile: same as adult of the same sex

Nest: cavity; female and male excavate; 1 brood per year

Eggs: 5-8; white without markings

Incubation: 11-14 days; female and male incubate

Fledging: 25-28 days; female and male feed young

Migration: non-migrator to partial in Wyoming

Food: insects, especially ants and beetles

Compare: Female Williamson's Sapsucker (pg. 59) has a finely barred back with a yellow belly and lacks Flicker's black spots on chest and belly. Look for Flicker's speckled breast and gray head to help identify.

Stan's Notes: This is the only woodpecker to regularly feed on the ground. Produces an antacid saliva that neutralizes the acidic defense of its ant prey. Male often picks the nest site; parents take up to 12 days to excavate a hole. Can be attracted with a nest box stuffed with sawdust; will often reuse an old nest. Male red-shafted has a red mustache; male yellow-shafted has a black mustache. Yellow-shafteds have golden yellow wing linings and tails. Hybrids between varieties occur in the Great Plains, where the ranges overlap. Undulates deeply in flight, calling "wacka-wacka" loudly. Look in wooded areas in lower elevations in the parks.

155

Mourning Dove
Zenaida macroura

YEAR-ROUND
SUMMER

Size: 12" (30 cm)

Male: Smooth fawn-colored dove. Gray patch on the head. Iridescent pink and greenish blue on neck. Single black spot behind and below eyes. Black spots on wings and tail. Pointed wedge-shaped tail with white edges.

Female: similar to male, lacking iridescent pink and green neck feathers

Juvenile: spotted and streaked

Nest: platform; female and male build; 2 broods per year

Eggs: 2; white without markings

Incubation: 13-14 days; male and female incubate, male incubates during the day, female at night

Fledging: 12-14 days; female and male feed young

Migration: complete to non-migrator in Wyoming

Food: seeds; will visit seed and ground feeders

Compare: Lacks the black collar and squared tail of the Eurasian Collared-Dove (pg. 255). Smaller than the Rock Pigeon (pg. 257) and lacks its wide range of color combinations.

Stan's Notes: Name comes from its mournful cooing. A ground feeder, bobbing its head as it walks. One of the few birds to drink without lifting its head, same as Rock Pigeon. Parents feed young (squab) a regurgitated liquid called crop-milk the first few days of life. Flimsy platform nest of twigs often falls apart in storms. Wind rushing through its wing feathers during takeoff and flight creates a characteristic whistling sound.

winter

breeding

Pied-billed Grebe
Podilymbus podiceps

SUMMER

Size: 13" (33 cm)

Male: Small brown water bird with a black chin and black ring around a thick, chicken-like ivory bill. Puffy white patch under the tail. Has an unmarked brown bill during winter.

Female: same as male

Juvenile: paler than adult, with white spots and gray chest, belly and bill

Nest: floating platform; female and male construct; 1 brood per year

Eggs: 5-7; bluish white without markings

Incubation: 22-24 days; female and male incubate

Fledging: 45-60 days; female and male feed young

Migration: complete, to southwestern states, Mexico and Central America

Food: crayfish, aquatic insects, fish

Compare: Look for a puffy white patch under the tail and thick, chicken-like bill to help identify.

Stan's Notes: A common water bird, often seen diving for food. Slowly sinks like a submarine if disturbed. Sinks without diving by quickly compressing its feathers to force out the air. Was called Hell-diver because of the length of time it can stay submerged. Can surface far from where it went under. Very sensitive to pollution. Well suited to life on water, with short wings, lobed toes, and legs set close to the rear of its body. While swimming is easy, it is very awkward on land. Builds nest on a floating mat in water. "Grebe" is likely from the Old English *krib*, meaning "crest," and refers to the crested head plumes of many grebes, especially during breeding season. Check ponds along Slough Creek Drive.

159

female

male pg. 67

Bufflehead
Bucephala albeola

YEAR-ROUND
MIGRATION
WINTER

Size: 13-15" (33-38 cm)

Female: Brownish gray duck with a dark brown head. White patch on cheek, just behind eyes.

Male: striking black and white duck, head shines green purple in sunlight, large white bonnet-like patch on back of head

Juvenile: similar to female

Nest: cavity; female lines an old woodpecker cavity; 1 brood per year

Eggs: 8-10; ivory to olive without markings

Incubation: 29-31 days; female incubates

Fledging: 50-55 days; female leads young to food

Migration: partial to non-migrator in Wyoming

Food: aquatic insects

Compare: Female Lesser Scaup (pg. 171) is larger and has a white patch at the base of its bill unlike the white cheek patch of female Bufflehead.

Stan's Notes: This very small, common duck is almost always in small groups or with other ducks. Seen on rivers and lakes in the state. Nests in old woodpecker holes. Known to use a burrow in an earthen bank when tree cavities are scarce. Will use a nest box. Uses down feathers to line the nest cavity. Unlike other ducks, the young remain in the nest for up to two days before venturing out with their mothers. Female is very territorial and stays with the same mate for many years. Found at many of the larger bodies of water in the parks. Check Fishing and Pelican Bridges. This is a diving duck, spending a couple minutes underwater, so be sure to watch for it long enough.

winter male

male

female

Ruddy Duck
Oxyura jamaicensis

SUMMER

Size: 15" (38 cm)

Male: Compact reddish brown body with a black crown and nape. Large bright white cheek patch. Distinctive light blue bill. Long tail, often raised above the water. Winter has a dull brown-to-gray body and dark bill.

Female: similar to winter male, lacks the large white cheek patch and blue bill

Juvenile: similar to female

Nest: ground; female builds; 1 brood per year

Eggs: 6-8; pale white without markings

Incubation: 23-26 days; female incubates

Fledging: 42-48 days; female and male feed young

Migration: complete, to Texas, southwestern states and Mexico

Food: aquatic insects and plants

Compare: Look for a light blue bill and raised tail to help identify the male Ruddy Duck.

Stan's Notes: A diving duck with a unique appearance. Awkward on land. Often secretive, found on ponds and bays. Flushes out quickly and stays away for a long time. Breeding male displays like a wind-up toy, ratcheting his head up and down, making muffled sounds and giving a staccato "pop." The male breeds with more than one female. Female lays some eggs in the nests of other ducks. A male is usually seen with a female and ducklings, but it may not be the father. Babies can dive soon after hatching. Has a blue bill, but this duck is not the species that duck hunters call Blue Bill.

male

female

Green-winged Teal
Anas crecca

YEAR-ROUND

Size: 15" (38 cm)

Male: A chestnut head with a dark green patch in back of eyes extending down to the nape of neck and outlined in white. Gray body. Butter yellow tail. Green patch on wings (speculum), seen in flight.

Female: light brown duck with black spots and green speculum, small black bill

Juvenile: same as female

Nest: ground; female builds; 1 brood per year

Eggs: 8-10; creamy white without markings

Incubation: 21-23 days; female incubates

Fledging: 32-34 days; female teaches young to feed

Migration: partial to non-migrator in Wyoming

Food: aquatic plants and insects

Compare: Female Blue-winged Teal (pg. 167) is similar in size, but it has slight white at the base of the bill. Look for a dark green patch on each side of a chestnut head to identify the male Green-winged Teal.

Stan's Notes: One of the smallest dabbling ducks, it tips forward in the water to feed off the bottom of shallow ponds. This behavior makes it vulnerable to ingesting spent lead shot, which can cause death. It walks well on land and also feeds in fields and woodlands. Known for its fast and agile flight, groups spin and wheel through the air in tight formation. Green speculum on wings most obvious in flight.

male

female

Blue-winged Teal
Spatula discors

SUMMER

Size: 15-16" (38-40 cm)

Male: Small, plain-looking brown duck with black speckles. Large white crescent-shaped mark at the base of bill. Gray head. Black tail with a small white patch. Blue wing patch (speculum), usually seen only in flight.

Female: duller version of male, lacks a crescent mark on the face and white patch on tail, showing only slight white at the base of bill

Juvenile: same as female

Nest: ground; female builds; 1 brood per year

Eggs: 8-11; creamy white

Incubation: 23-27 days; female incubates

Fledging: 35-44 days; female feeds young

Migration: complete, to southwestern states, Mexico and Central America

Food: aquatic plants, seeds, aquatic insects

Compare: The female Green-winged Teal (pg. 165) has a similar size, but it lacks white at the base of its bill. The female Mallard (pg. 187) is larger. Look for the distinctive white facial marking to help identify the male Blue-winged Teal.

Stan's Notes: One of the smallest ducks in North America and one of the longest distance migrating ducks. Widespread nesting, as far north as Alaska. Builds nest some distance from the water. Female performs a distraction display to protect the nest and young. Male leaves the female near the end of incubation. Planting crops and cultivating to pond edges have caused declining populations.

Cinnamon Teal
Spatula cyanoptera

MIGRATION
SUMMER

Size: 16" (40 cm)

Male: Deep cinnamon head, neck and belly. Light brown back. Dark gray bill. Deep red eyes. Non-breeding (July to September) male is overall brown with a red tinge.

Female: overall brown with a pale brown head, long shovel-like bill, green patch on wings

Juvenile: similar to female

Nest: ground; female builds; 1 brood per year

Eggs: 7-12; pinkish white without markings

Incubation: 21-25 days; female incubates

Fledging: 40-50 days; female teaches young to feed

Migration: complete, to southwestern states and Mexico

Food: aquatic plants and insects, seeds

Compare: Male Teal shares the cinnamon sides of the larger male Northern Shoveler (pg. 285), but lacks the Shoveler's green head and very large spoon-shaped bill. Female Cinnamon Teal looks very similar to the smaller female Green-winged Teal (pg. 165), which has a dark line through its eyes.

Stan's Notes: The male is one of the most stunningly beautiful ducks. When threatened, the female feigns a wing injury to lure the predator away from her young. Prefers to nest along alkaline marshes and shallow lakes, within 75 yards (68 m) of the water. Mallards and other ducks often lay eggs in teal nests, resulting in many nests with over 15 eggs. Slough Creek Drive is well known for Cinnamon Teals. Yellowstone Lake, Jackson Lake and several large, slow-moving rivers are good places for this duck.

169

male pg. 69

female

Lesser Scaup
Aythya affinis

MIGRATION
SUMMER

Size: 16-17" (40-43 cm)

Female: Overall brown duck with a dull white patch at the base of a light gray bill. Yellow eyes.

Male: white and gray duck, chest and head appear nearly black but the head looks purple with green highlights in direct sun, yellow eyes

Juvenile: same as female

Nest: ground; female builds; 1 brood per year

Eggs: 8-14; olive buff without markings

Incubation: 22-28 days; female incubates

Fledging: 45-50 days; female teaches young to feed

Migration: complete, to southwestern states, Mexico and Central America

Food: aquatic plants and insects

Compare: Male Blue-winged Teal (pg. 167) is slightly smaller and has a crescent-shaped white mark at the base of its bill.

Stan's Notes: A common diving duck. Often seen in large flocks on lakes, ponds and sewage lagoons. Submerges itself completely to feed on the bottom of lakes (unlike dabbling ducks, which only tip forward to reach the bottom). Note the bold white stripe under the wings when in flight. Male leaves the female when she starts incubating eggs. The quantity of eggs (clutch size) increases with the age of the female. This species has an interesting baby-sitting arrangement in which groups of young (crèches) are tended by 1-3 adult females. Check Junction Butte Ponds.

Short-eared Owl
Asio flammeus

YEAR-ROUND

Size: 14½-17½" (37-44 cm); up to 3¾-ft. wingspan

Male: Overall brown to gray with a large round head and light face. Heavy streaking on the chest with a lighter belly. Spotted back. Black "wrist" mark. Very short, tiny ear tufts, often not noticeable. Bright yellow eyes and dark eye patches.

Female: same as male, but overall darker

Juvenile: similar to adults, light gray with a dark face

Nest: ground; depression scraped just deep enough to stop the eggs from rolling away; 1 brood per year

Eggs: 4-7 eggs; white without markings

Incubation: 26-30 days; female incubates

Fledging: 23-36 days; male and female feed young

Migration: non-migrator to partial in Wyoming

Food: small mammals, birds

Compare: Hard to confuse with the much larger Great Horned Owl (pg. 207), which has large feather tufts on its head. Stiff wing beats and erratic flight make the Short-eared Owl easy to identify.

Stan's Notes: Hunts over open fields, often floating on its long wings just before dropping onto prey. Flies with long, slow wing beats. The male calls while soaring high above the nest site, sometimes swooping and clapping its wings together beneath its body. Perches on the ground. Distinctive black "wrist" mark under wings and a bold tan patch near the upper end of wings, seen in flight.

in flight
male

in flight
female

juvenile

Prairie Falcon
Falco mexicanus

YEAR-ROUND

Size: 15-18" (38-45 cm); up to 3¾-foot wingspan

Male: Thin body with a pale brown head, back and tail. White breast and underwings with small brown spots. Black armpits with black speckling extending onto wing linings. Large squared head with a white area behind eyes. Dark narrow mustache markings. Yellow base of bill, eye-rings, legs and feet.

Female: noticeably larger than male, with a heavier, nearly black patch on underwings

Juvenile: overall darker than adults, with heavy streaks on chest and belly and nearly black armpits

Nest: scrape, on a cliff ledge or bluff face; adult scrapes away loose dirt; 1 brood per year

Eggs: 4-5; white with brown markings

Incubation: 29-31 days; male and female incubate

Fledging: 35-42 days; male and female feed young

Migration: non-migrator; moves around to find food

Food: birds, insects, small mammals and reptiles

Compare: Much larger than American Kestrel (pg. 149) and lacks the rusty back and tail.

Stan's Notes: A falcon of open prairies in Wyoming. Perches on telephone poles, cliffs or hovers in search of prey. Jumps from a perch in a burst of rapid flight to overtake birds flying low to the ground. When soaring it dives from high up, knocking small birds out of the sky to the ground. During courtship the male performs a strutting display for the female on the edge of the nest along with spectacular aerial displays, all while calling to her. In proportion to its head, its eyes are larger than those of any other falcon.

displaying

non-displaying

Sharp-tailed Grouse
Tympanuchus phasianellus

YEAR-ROUND

Size: 16-18" (40-45 cm); up to 2-foot wingspan

Male: Overall brown grouse with white and dark brown-to-black marks. Paler below. Yellow eyebrows (combs). Pale purple throat sacs. Small crest. A narrow, pointed white tail.

Female: similar to non-displaying male

Juvenile: similar to female

Nest: ground; female builds; 1 brood per year

Eggs: 5-15; light brown with brown markings

Incubation: 21-24 days; female incubates

Fledging: 7-10 days; female leads young to food

Migration: non-migrator; moves around to find food

Food: seeds, nuts, insects, berries, leaves

Compare: Similar size as the Ruffed Grouse (pg. 179), which has a squared dark tail. The female Ring-necked Pheasant (pg. 211) is larger, has a longer tail and lacks the crest. Look for the narrow, pointed white tail to help identify the Sharp-tailed Grouse.

Stan's Notes: An upland game species named for its pointed tail. Males gather in groups of up to 20 birds in an area called a lek to dance and display. Leks are often used for many years. Displaying males bow forward, droop their wings at their sides and point their tails straight up in the air. Appearing like wind-up toys, they stamp their feet quickly and produce a loud rattling noise that resonates from the throat sac, which is inflated with air. Females choose the best dancers, which tend to be the older, more experienced males. Often these males are in the center of the group.

drumming

Ruffed Grouse
Bonasa umbellus

YEAR-ROUND

Size: 16-19" (40-48 cm); up to 2-foot wingspan

Male: Brown chicken-like bird with a long squared tail. Wide black band near tip of tail. Is able to fan tail like a turkey. Tuft of feathers on the head stands like a crown. Black ruffs on sides of neck.

Female: same as male, but less obvious neck ruffs

Juvenile: same as female

Nest: ground; female builds; 1 brood per year

Eggs: 9-12; tan with light brown markings

Incubation: 23-24 days; female incubates

Fledging: 10-12 days; female leads young to food

Migration: non-migrator; moves around to find food

Food: seeds, insects, fruit, leaf buds

Compare: Female Ring-necked Pheasant (pg. 211) is larger and has a longer, pointed tail. Look for a feathered tuft on the head and black neck ruffs to help identify the Ruffed Grouse.

Stan's Notes: A common bird in some areas. Often seen in aspen or other trees, feeding on leaf buds. In the more northern climates, bristles grow on its feet in winter, which serve as snowshoes. When there is enough snow, it will dive into a snowbank to roost at night. In spring, the male raises its crest (tuft), fans tail feathers and stands on logs, drumming with its wings to attract females. The drumming sound comes from its cupped wings moving air, not from pounding against its chest or a log. Female performs a distraction display to protect her young. Two color morphs, red and gray, most apparent in the tail. Black ruffs on the neck gave rise to its common name.

female

male pg. 265

Dusky Grouse
Dendragapus obscurus

YEAR-ROUND

Size: 19" (48 cm)

Female: Mottled, chicken-like brown bird with a gray belly. Yellow patch of skin above eyes (comb) is less obvious than the male's comb. Tail is darker brown and squared off.

Male: dark gray bird with bright yellow-to-orange patch of skin above eyes (comb)

Juvenile: similar to female

Nest: ground; female builds; 1 brood per year

Eggs: 6-12; pale white with brown markings

Incubation: 24-26 days; female incubates

Fledging: 7-10 days; female feeds young

Migration: non-migrator; will move around to find food

Food: insects, seeds, fruit, leaf buds and coniferous needles (Douglas-fir)

Compare: The Ruffed Grouse (pg. 179) is lighter brown. Sharp-tailed Grouse (pg. 177) has a pointed white tail. The female Ring-necked Pheasant (pg. 211) is larger and has a longer tail.

Stan's Notes: The most common grouse of the Rockies, found from the foothills to the timberline. Usually on the ground but also in trees during spring, feeding on newly opened leaf buds. Often switches from an insect diet in summer to coniferous needles in winter. Male engages in elaborate courtship displays by fanning its tail, inflating its bright neck sac and singing (calling). Male mates with several females. Young leave the nest within 24 hours after hatching and follow their mothers to feed. Very tame and freezes if threatened, making it easy to get a close look. Hike trails, wooded ridges and mid-elevations in the parks to see this bird.

male pg. 301

female

Redhead
Aythya americana

Size: 19" (48 cm)

Female: A soft brown plain-looking duck with gray-to-white wing linings. Rounded top of head. Two-toned bill, gray with a black tip.

Male: rich red head and neck with a black chest and tail, gray sides, smoky gray wings and back, tricolored bill with a light blue base, white ring and black tip

Juvenile: similar to female

Nest: cup; female builds; 1 brood per year

Eggs: 9-14; pale white without markings

Incubation: 24-28 days; female and male incubate

Fledging: 56-73 days; female shows young what to eat

Migration: complete, to southwestern states, Mexico and Central America

Food: seeds, aquatic plants, insects

Compare: The female Northern Shoveler (pg. 189) is lighter brown in color with an exceptionally large, shovel-shaped bill.

Stan's Notes: A duck of permanent large bodies of water. Forages along the shoreline, feeding on seeds, aquatic plants and insects. Usually builds nest directly on the water's surface, using large mats of vegetation. Female lays up to 75 percent of its eggs in the nests of other Redheads and several other duck species. Nests primarily in the Prairie Pothole region of the northern Great Plains. Overall populations seem to be increasing at about 2-3 percent each year.

male pg. 73

female

Common Goldeneye
Bucephala clangula

WINTER

Size: 18½-20" (47-50 cm)

Female: A brown and gray duck with a large dark brown head and gray body. White collar. Bright golden eyes. Yellow-tipped dark bill.

Male: mostly white duck with a black back and a large, puffy green head, large white spot in front of each bright golden eye, dark bill

Juvenile: same as female, but has a dark bill

Nest: cavity; female lines an old woodpecker cavity; 1 brood per year

Eggs: 8-10; light green without markings

Incubation: 28-32 days; female incubates

Fledging: 56-59 days; female leads young to food

Migration: complete, to Wyoming, southwestern states and Mexico

Food: aquatic plants, insects, fish, mollusks

Compare: Female Lesser Scaup (pg. 171) has a white patch at the base of its bill. Look for the large dark brown head and white collar to identify the female Common Goldeneye.

Stan's Notes: Known for its loud whistling in flight, produced by its wings. In late winter and early spring, the male often attracts a female through elaborate displays, throwing his head back while uttering a raspy note. Female will lay eggs in other goldeneye nests, resulting in some mothers incubating up to 30 eggs. Received the common name from its obvious bright golden eyes. Can be seen in both parks on larger bodies of water, such as Yellowstone Lake, Jackson Lake, Lewis Lake and Twin Lakes.

male pg. 287

female

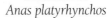

Mallard
Anas platyrhynchos

YEAR-ROUND

Size: 19-21" (48-53 cm)

Female: Brown duck with an orange and black bill and blue and white wing mark (speculum).

Male: large, bulbous green head, white necklace, rust brown or chestnut chest, combination of gray and white on the sides, yellow bill, orange legs and feet

Juvenile: same as female, but with a yellow bill

Nest: ground; female builds; 1 brood per year

Eggs: 7-10; greenish to whitish, unmarked

Incubation: 26-30 days; female incubates

Fledging: 42-52 days; female leads young to food

Migration: partial to non-migrator in Wyoming; moves around to find open water and food in winter

Food: seeds, plants, aquatic insects; will come to ground feeders offering corn

Compare: The female Northern Shoveler (pg. 189) is smaller and has a large spoon-shaped bill. Female Northern Pintail (pg. 193) is similar, but it has a gray bill. The female Blue-winged Teal (pg. 167) is smaller than female Mallard.

Stan's Notes: A familiar duck of lakes and ponds, it's considered a type of dabbling duck, tipping forward in shallow water to feed on aquatic plants on the bottom. The name "Mallard" comes from the Latin *masculus*, meaning "male," referring to the habit of males not taking part in raising ducklings. Both female and male have white tails and white underwings. Black central tail feathers of male curl upward. Will return to place of birth.

male pg. 285

female

Northern Shoveler
Spatula clypeata

SUMMER

Size: 20" (50 cm)

Female: A medium-sized brown duck speckled with black. Green speculum. An extraordinarily large, spoon-shaped bill that is almost always held pointed toward the water.

Male: iridescent green head, rusty sides and white breast, spoon-shaped bill

Juvenile: same as female

Nest: ground; female builds; 1 brood per year

Eggs: 9-12; olive without markings

Incubation: 22-25 days; female incubates

Fledging: 30-60 days; female leads young to food

Migration: complete, to southwestern states, Mexico and Central America

Food: aquatic insects, plants

Compare: Similar color as female Mallard (pg. 187), but Mallard lacks the Shoveler's large bill. Look for the large spoon-shaped bill of Northern Shoveler to help identify.

Stan's Notes: Named for the peculiar shape of the bill. "Northern" in the common name was given because this is the only species of these ducks in North America. Found in small flocks of 5-10 birds, swimming low in water, pointing its large bill toward the water as if it's too heavy to lift. Feeds mainly by filtering tiny aquatic insects and plants from the water's surface with its bill, often swimming in tight circles while feeding. Check all large and small lakes in both parks for shovelers.

female

male pg. 267

Gadwall
Mareca strepera

YEAR-ROUND
SUMMER

Size: 20" (50 cm)

Female: Mottled brown with a pronounced change in color from a dark brown body to light brown neck and head. Bright white wing linings, seen in flight. Small white wing patch, seen when swimming. Gray bill with orange sides.

Male: plump gray duck with a brown head and distinctive black rump, white belly, bright white wing linings, small white wing patch, chestnut-tinged wings and a gray bill

Juvenile: similar to female

Nest: ground; female lines the nest with fine grass and down feathers plucked from her breast; 1 brood per year

Eggs: 8-11; white without markings

Incubation: 24-27 days; female incubates

Fledging: 48-56 days; young feed themselves

Migration: complete to non-migrator in Wyoming

Food: aquatic insects

Compare: The female Gadwall is very similar to the female Mallard (pg. 187). Look for the white wing patch and gray bill with orange sides to help identify the female Gadwall.

Stan's Notes: A duck of shallow marshes. Consumes mostly plant material, dunking its head in water to feed rather than tipping forward, like other dabbling ducks. Walks well on land; feeds in fields and woodlands. Frequently in pairs with other duck species. Nests within 300 feet (100 m) of water. Establishes pair bond in winter.

male

female

Northern Pintail
Anas acuta

YEAR-ROUND
SUMMER

Size: 20" (50 cm), female
25" (63 cm), male

Male: A slender, elegant duck with a brown head, white neck, gray body and extremely long, narrow black tail. Gray bill. Non-breeding has a pale brown head that lacks the clear demarcation between the brown head and white neck. Lacks long tail feathers.

Female: mottled brown body with a paler head and neck, long tail and gray bill

Juvenile: similar to female

Nest: ground; female builds; 1 brood per year

Eggs: 6-9; olive green without markings

Incubation: 22-25 days; female incubates

Fledging: 36-50 days; female teaches young to feed

Migration: complete to non-migrator in Wyoming

Food: aquatic plants and insects, seeds

Compare: The male Northern Pintail has a distinctive brown head and white neck. Look for the unique long tail feathers. The female Pintail is similar to the female Mallard (pg. 187), but Mallard has an orange bill with black spots.

Stan's Notes: A common dabbling duck of marshes in Wyoming. About 90 percent of its diet is aquatic plants, except when females feed heavily on aquatic insects before nesting, presumably to gain extra nutrients for egg production. Male holds his tail upright from the water's surface. No other North American duck has such a long tail. Look in larger lakes and ponds in the parks for this duck.

male pg. 303

female

Canvasback
Aythya valisineria

MIGRATION
SUMMER

Size: 20½" (52 cm)

Female: Brown head, neck and breast with light gray-to-brown sides. Long sloping forehead that transitions into a long dark bill.

Male: deep red head and neck, sloping forehead, long black bill, gray and white sides and back, black chest and tail

Juvenile: similar to female

Nest: ground; female builds; 1 brood per year

Eggs: 7-9; pale white to gray without markings

Incubation: 24-29 days; female incubates

Fledging: 56-67 days; female leads young to food

Migration: complete, to southwestern states and Mexico

Food: aquatic insects, small clams

Compare: Female Lesser Scaup (pg. 171) is smaller and has a white patch at the base of its bill; lacks the sloping forehead and long dark bill of the female Canvasback.

Stan's Notes: A large inland duck of freshwater lakes, rivers and ponds. Populations declined dramatically in the 1960-80s due to marsh drainage for agriculture. Females return to their birthplace (philopatric) while males disperse to new areas. Will mate during migration or on the breeding grounds. A courting male gives a soft cooing call when displaying and during aerial chases. Male leaves the female after incubation starts. Female takes a new mate every year. Female feeds very little during incubation and will lose up to 70 percent of fat reserves during that time. Yellowstone Lake and Jackson Lake are popular places to look for this waterfowl.

male
pg. 263

female

soaring

Northern Harrier
Circus hudsonius

YEAR-ROUND

Size: 18-22" (45-56 cm); up to 4-foot wingspan

Female: A slim, low-flying hawk. Dark brown back with a brown-streaked chest and belly. Large white rump patch and narrow black bands across tail. Black wing tips. Yellow eyes.

Male: silver gray with a large white rump patch and white belly, faint narrow bands across tail, black wing tips, yellow eyes

Juvenile: similar to female, with an orange chest

Nest: ground; female and male construct; 1 brood per year

Eggs: 4-8; bluish white without markings

Incubation: 31-32 days; female incubates

Fledging: 30-35 days; male and female feed young

Migration: non-migrator to partial in Wyoming

Food: mice, snakes, insects, small birds

Compare: Slimmer than the Red-tailed Hawk (pg. 203). Look for black tail bands, a white rump patch and the characteristic flight to help identify.

Stan's Notes: One of the easiest of hawks to identify. Glides near the ground, following the contours of the land while searching for prey. Holds its wings just above a horizontal position, tilting back and forth in the wind, similar to Turkey Vultures. Formerly called Marsh Hawk due to its habit of hunting over marshes. Feeds on the ground. Will perch on the ground to preen and rest. Unlike other hawks, uses its hearing primarily to locate prey, followed by eyesight. At any age, it has a distinctive owl-like face disk. Look for it in Hayden and Lamar Valleys in Yellowstone. Also along the road just outside Jenny Lake Campground in the Tetons.

197

dark morph

light morph

soaring dark morph

soaring light morph

Rough-legged Hawk
Buteo lagopus

WINTER

Size: 18-23" (45-58 cm); up to 4½-foot wingspan

Male: A hawk of several plumages. All have a long tail with a dark band or bands, relatively long wings, and a small bill and feet. Distinctive dark "wrists" and belly. Light morph has a nearly pure white underside of wings and base of tail. Dark morph is nearly all brown with a light gray trailing edge of wings.

Female: same as male, only larger

Juvenile: same as adults

Nest: platform, on edge of cliff; female and male build; 1 brood per year

Eggs: 2-6; white without markings

Incubation: 28-31 days; female and male incubate

Fledging: 39-43 days; female and male feed young

Migration: complete, to Wyoming and the northern half of the U.S.

Food: small mammals, snakes, large insects

Compare: Red-tailed Hawk (pg. 203) has a belly band and lacks dark "wrist" marks. The Osprey (pg. 81) has similar dark "wrists," but lacks the dark belly of the Rough-legged Hawk.

Stan's Notes: Two color morphs; light is more common than the dark. A common resident during winter, nesting in the Canadian Northwest Territories and Alaska. More numerous in some years than in others. It has much smaller, weaker feet than other birds of prey and must hunt smaller prey. Hunts from the air, usually hovering before diving for mice, voles and other small rodents.

soaring light morph

intermediate morph

light morph

dark morph

soaring dark morph

Swainson's Hawk
Buteo swainsoni

MIGRATION
SUMMER

Size: 19-22" (48-56 cm); up to 4¾-foot wingspan

Male: A highly variable-plumaged hawk with three easily distinguishable color morphs. The light morph is brown and has a white belly, warm rusty chest and white face. The intermediate has a dark chest, rusty belly and white at the base of bill. The dark morph is nearly all dark brown with a rusty color low on the belly.

Female: same as male

Juvenile: similar to adult

Nest: platform; female and male construct; 1 brood per year

Eggs: 2-4; bluish or white with some brown marks

Incubation: 28-35 days; female and male incubate

Fledging: 28-30 days; female and male feed young

Migration: complete, to Central and South America

Food: small mammals, insects, snakes, birds

Compare: Slimmer than Red-tailed Hawk (pg. 203) and has longer, more pointed wings and a longer tail. Ferruginous Hawk (pg. 209) has a light trailing edge of wings. Rough-legged Hawk (pg. 199) has a lighter trailing edge of wings.

Stan's Notes: A slender open country hawk that hunts mammals, insects, snakes and birds when soaring (kiting) or perching. Often flies with slightly upturned wings in a teetering, vulture-like flight. The light morph is the most common, but the intermediate and dark are also common. Even minor nest disturbance can cause nest failure. Often gathers in large flocks to migrate. Look in Hayden Valley for this raptor during summer and migration.

soaring

Western

Eastern

soaring

Red-tailed Hawk
Buteo jamaicensis

YEAR-ROUND
SUMMER

Size: 19-23" (48-58 cm); up to 4½-foot wingspan

Male: A large hawk with a wide variety of colors from bird to bird, from chocolate brown to nearly all white. Often brown with a white breast and distinctive brown belly band. Rust red tail, usually seen only from above. Wing underside is white with a small dark patch on leading edge near shoulder.

Female: same as male, only slightly larger

Juvenile: similar to adults, lacking the red tail, has a speckled chest and light eyes

Nest: platform; male and female construct; 1 brood per year

Eggs: 2-3; white without markings or sometimes marked with brown

Incubation: 30-35 days; female and male incubate

Fledging: 45-46 days; male and female feed young

Migration: partial to non-migrator in Wyoming

Food: mice, birds, snakes, insects, mammals

Compare: Swainson's Hawk (pg. 201) is slimmer with longer, more pointed wings and a longer tail.

Stan's Notes: Common hawk of open country and in cities, often perching on freeway light posts, fences and trees. Circles over open fields and roadsides, searching for prey. Builds a large stick nest; commonly seen in large trees along roads. Lines the nest with finer material such as evergreen tree needles. Returns to same nest site each year. Develops the red tail in its second year. Western variety has a brown chin; Eastern's is white. Map reflects the combined range. Lamar Valley is a good place to search for Red-tails.

203

winter

breeding

in flight

White-faced Ibis
Plegadis chihi

MIGRATION
SUMMER

Size: 23" (58 cm); up to 3-foot wingspan

Male: Appears brown with rusty red (chestnut) on upper body. Glossy brown with a green sheen on lower body. Long, down-curved gray bill. White border on a light red face. Orange-red legs and feet. Deep red eyes. Winter has a gray mask and less chestnut.

Female: same as male

Juvenile: similar to winter adult

Nest: platform, on ground, low in a shrub or small tree; female and male build; 1 brood per year

Eggs: 2-4; blue or green with brown markings

Incubation: 21-23 days; female and male incubate

Fledging: 30-35 days; female and male feed young

Migration: complete, to southwestern states and Mexico

Food: insects, crayfish, frogs, small fish, shellfish

Compare: American Avocet (pg. 71) is mostly black and white with an upturned bill.

Stan's Notes: Usually found in marshes. When it is near, in good light it appears glossy red with green, blue and purple highlights. Uses its long bill to locate and eat aquatic insects and fish. Large groups fly in a straight line. Rapid, shallow wing beats, then a short glide. Nests close to water in large colonies with egrets and herons. Builds a loose nest of thin twigs, leaves and roots, lined with green leaves. Common name comes from the white outline on its face.

Great Horned Owl
Bubo virginianus

YEAR-ROUND

Size: 21-25" (53-63 cm); up to 3½-foot wingspan

Male: A robust brown "horned" owl. Bright yellow eyes and V-shaped white throat resembling a necklace. Horizontal barring on the chest.

Female: same as male, only slightly larger

Juvenile: similar to adults, lacking ear tufts

Nest: no nest; takes over the nest of a crow, Great Blue Heron or hawk, or uses a partial cavity, stump or broken-off tree; 1 brood per year

Eggs: 2-3; white without markings

Incubation: 26-30 days; female incubates

Fledging: 30-35 days; male and female feed young

Migration: non-migrator

Food: mammals, birds (ducks), snakes, insects

Compare: The Short-eared Owl (pg. 173) lacks obvious "horns" on its head. Look for bright yellow eyes and large tufts of feathers on the head to help identify the Great Horned Owl.

Stan's Notes: This owl is a winter nester, laying eggs in January and February. It has excellent hearing; able to hear a mouse move beneath a pile of leaves or a foot of snow. "Ears" are tufts of feathers (horns) and have nothing to do with hearing. Not able to turn its head all the way around. Wing feathers are ragged on the ends, resulting in silent flight. Eyelids close from the top down, like humans. Fearless, it's one of the few animals that will kill a skunk or porcupine. Because of this, it is sometimes called Flying Tiger. Look for Great Horns in any of the campgrounds in the parks with large cottonwood trees.

soaring

soaring
juvenile

juvenile

Ferruginous Hawk
Buteo regalis

MIGRATION
SUMMER

Size: 22-26" (56-66 cm); up to 4½-foot wingspan

Male: A pale brown head, gray cheeks and reddish back. White chin, chest and belly. Rust flanks extend down rust feathered legs. Bright white undersides of wings, light rust wing linings. Tail white below, rust-tinged on top. Large, strong yellow feet. Red eyes. Dark eye line.

Female: same as male, but noticeably larger

Juvenile: brown head, nape of neck, back and wings, white chin, chest and belly

Nest: massive platform, low in a tree, sometimes on the ground; female and male build; 1 brood per year

Eggs: 2-4; bluish or white, can have brown marks

Incubation: 28-33 days; female and male incubate

Fledging: 44-48 days; female and male feed young

Migration: complete, to southwestern states and Mexico

Food: larger mammals, snakes, insects, birds

Compare: Swainson's Hawk (pg. 201) is smaller and has a dark trailing edge of wings. Red-tailed Hawk (pg. 203) has a brown belly band and lacks the rust flanks and legs of Ferruginous.

Stan's Notes: The largest hawk species. Found in western states. Common name means "iron-like," referring to the rusty color on its legs. Male and female perform a soaring aerial courtship, holding their wings above their backs. Male dives toward the female, and they grab each other with their large, powerful feet. Often hunts larger mammals such as jackrabbits. Often stands on the ground. Look in Hayden and Lamar Valleys for this raptor.

male

female

Ring-necked Pheasant
Phasianus colchicus

YEAR-ROUND

Size: 30-36" (76-90 cm), male, including tail
21-25" (53-63 cm), female, including tail

Male: Golden brown body with a long tail. White ring around the neck. Head is purple, green, blue and red.

Female: smaller, less flamboyant all-brown bird with a long tail

Juvenile: similar to female, with a shorter tail

Nest: ground; female builds; 1 brood per year

Eggs: 8-10; olive brown without markings

Incubation: 23-25 days; female incubates

Fledging: 11-12 days; female leads young to food

Migration: non-migrator; moves around to find food

Food: insects, seeds, fruit; visits ground feeders

Compare: Ruffed Grouse (pg. 179) is smaller, with a feathered tuft on its head and black ruffs on the neck; lacks the long pointed tail of female Ring-necked. The male Ring-necked is much larger than the female. Both have long tails, but the male is brightly colored.

Stan's Notes: Originally introduced to North America from China in the late 1800s. Common now throughout the United States. Like many other game birds, its numbers vary greatly, making it common during some years and scarce in others. Common name "Ring-necked" refers to the thin white ring around the male's neck. "Pheasant" comes from the Greek *phaisianos*, meaning "bird of the River Phasis." (This river is located in Europe and is now known as the Rioni River.) Listen for the male's cackling call, which attracts females. Roosts on the ground or in trees at night.

soaring

soaring
juvenile

juvenile

Golden Eagle
Aquila chrysaetos

YEAR-ROUND

Size: 30-40" (76-102 cm); up to 7¼-foot wingspan

Male: Uniform dark brown with a golden yellow head and nape of neck. Yellow around base of bill. Yellow feet.

Female: same as male

Juvenile: similar to adult, with white "wrist" patches and a white base of tail

Nest: platform, on a cliff; female and male build; 1 brood per year

Eggs: 1-2; white with brown markings

Incubation: 43-45 days; female and male incubate

Fledging: 63-75 days; female and male feed young

Migration: non-migrator to partial in Wyoming; moves around to find food

Food: mammals, birds, reptiles, insects

Compare: The Bald Eagle (pg. 83) adult is similar, but it has a white head and white tail. Bald Eagle juvenile is often confused with the Golden Eagle juvenile; both are large dark birds with white markings.

Stan's Notes: A large, powerful raptor that has no trouble taking larger prey such as jackrabbits. Hunts by perching or soaring and watching for movement. Inhabits mountainous terrain, requiring large territories to provide a large supply of food. Long-term pair bond, renewing its bond late in winter with spectacular high-flying courtship displays. Usually nests on cliff faces; rarely nests in trees. Uses a well-established nest that's been used for generations. Will add items to the nest such as antlers, bones and barbed wire. Lamar Valley near Soda Butte is a good place for Golden Eagles.

displaying male

non-displaying

female

Wild Turkey
Meleagris gallopavo

YEAR-ROUND

Size: 36-48" (90-120 cm)

Male: Large, plump brown and bronze bird with a striking blue and red bare head. Fan tail and a long, straight black beard in center of chest. Spurs on legs.

Female: thinner and less striking than male, usually lacking a breast beard

Juvenile: same as adult of the same sex

Nest: ground; female builds; 1 brood per year

Eggs: 10-12; buff white with dull brown markings

Incubation: 27-28 days; female incubates

Fledging: 6-10 days; female leads young to food

Migration: non-migrator; moves around to find food

Food: insects, seeds, fruit

Compare: This bird is quite distinctive and unlikely to be confused with others.

Stan's Notes: This is the largest native game bird in Wyoming, and the species from which the domestic turkey was bred. It almost became our national bird, losing to the Bald Eagle by one vote. Eliminated from many western states due to market hunting and loss of habitat. Reintroduced widely during the 1960-80s. Populations now stable. A strong flier that can approach 60 mph (97 km/h). Able to fly straight up, then away. Eyesight is three times better than human eyesight. Hearing is also excellent; can hear competing males up to a mile away. Males hold "harems" of up to 20 females. Males are known as toms, females are hens, young are poults. Roosts in trees at night.

male

female

Golden-crowned Kinglet
Regulus satrapa

YEAR-ROUND
WINTER

Size: 4" (10 cm)

Male: Tiny, plump green-to-gray bird. Distinctive yellow and orange patch with a black border on the crown (see inset). A white eyebrow mark. Two white wing bars.

Female: same as male, but has a yellow crown with a black border, lacks any orange (see inset)

Juvenile: same as adults, but lacks gold on crown

Nest: pendulous; female builds; 1-2 broods per year

Eggs: 5-9; white or creamy with brown markings

Incubation: 14-15 days; female incubates

Fledging: 14-19 days; female and male feed young

Migration: non-migrator to partial in Wyoming

Food: insects, fruit, tree sap

Compare: Similar to Ruby-crowned Kinglet (pg. 219), but Golden-crowned has an obvious crown. Smaller than the female American Goldfinch (pg. 317), which has an all-black forehead.

Stan's Notes: Common year-round resident in parts of Wyoming, but it might be seen more often during migration, when flocks from farther north move through. Often in flocks with chickadees, nuthatches, woodpeckers and Ruby-crowned Kinglets. Flicks its wings when moving around. Constructs an unusual hanging nest, often with moss, lichens and spider webs, and lines it with bark and feathers. Can have so many eggs in its small nest that eggs are in two layers. Drinks tree sap and feeds by gleaning insects from trees. Can be very tame and approachable.

Ruby-crowned Kinglet
Regulus calendula

Size: 4" (10 cm)

Male: A small, teardrop-shaped green-to-gray bird. Two white wing bars and a white eye-ring. Hidden ruby crown.

Female: same as male, but lacking the ruby crown

Juvenile: same as female

Nest: pendulous; female builds; 1 brood per year

Eggs: 4-5; white with brown markings

Incubation: 11-12 days; female incubates

Fledging: 11-12 days; female and male feed young

Migration: complete, to southwestern states, Mexico and Central America

Food: insects, berries

Compare: Golden-crowned Kinglet (pg. 217) lacks the ruby crown. The female American Goldfinch (pg. 317) shares the same olive color and unmarked breast, but it is larger. Look for the white eye-ring of Ruby-crowned Kinglet.

Stan's Notes: One of the smaller birds found in Wyoming. Most commonly seen during migration, when groups travel together. Watch for it flitting around thick shrubs low to the ground. It takes a quick eye to see the male's ruby crown. Female constructs an unusual pendulous (sac-like) nest, intricately woven and decorated on the outside with colored lichens and mosses stuck together with spider webs. Nest is suspended from a branch overlapped by leaves and usually is hung high in a mature tree. The name "Kinglet" originates from the Anglo-Saxon word *cyning*, or "king," referring to the male's ruby crown, and the diminutive suffix "let," meaning "small."

male

female

Red-breasted Nuthatch
Sitta canadensis

YEAR-ROUND

Size: 4½" (11 cm)

Male: Small gray-backed bird with a black cap and prominent eye line. Rust red chest and belly.

Female: gray cap, pale undersides

Juvenile: same as female

Nest: cavity; male and female excavate; 1 brood per year

Eggs: 5-6; white with red brown markings

Incubation: 11-12 days; female incubates

Fledging: 14-20 days; female and male feed young

Migration: non-migrator to irruptive; will move around in search of food

Food: insects, seeds; visits seed and suet feeders

Compare: Smaller than the White-breasted Nuthatch (pg. 229), with a red chest instead of white.

Stan's Notes: The Red-breasted Nuthatch behaves like the White-breasted Nuthatch, climbing down tree trunks headfirst. Similar to chickadees, visits seed feeders, quickly grabbing a seed and flying off to crack it open. Will wedge a seed into a crevice and pound it open with several sharp blows. The name "Nuthatch" comes from the Middle English moniker *nuthak*, referring to the bird's habit of wedging a seed into a crevice and hacking it open. Look for it in mature conifers, where it often extracts seeds from cones. Excavates a cavity or takes an old woodpecker hole or natural cavity and constructs a nest. Irruptive migration means the bird is common in some winters and scarce in others. Check stands of evergreens near Mammoth Campground in Yellowstone. Also look above the Upper Terrace.

Black-capped Chickadee
Poecile atricapillus

YEAR-ROUND

Size: 5" (13 cm)

Male: Familiar gray bird with a black cap and throat patch. White chest and tan belly. Small white wing marks.

Female: same as male

Juvenile: same as adult

Nest: cavity; female and male construct or excavate; 1 brood per year

Eggs: 5-7; white with fine brown markings

Incubation: 11-13 days; female and male incubate

Fledging: 14-18 days; female and male feed young

Migration: non-migrator

Food: insects, seeds, fruit; will come to seed and suet feeders

Compare: Mountain Chickadee (pg. 225) is similar, but it has white eyebrows.

Stan's Notes: A backyard bird that is attracted with a nest box or seed feeder. Usually the first to find a new feeder. Can be easily tamed and hand fed. Much of its diet comes from bird feeders, so it can be a common urban bird. Needs to feed each day in winter; forages for food even in the worst winter storms. Often seen with nuthatches, woodpeckers and other birds. Builds nest mostly with green moss and lines it with fur. Named for its familiar "chika-dee-dee-dee-dee" call. Also calls a high-pitched, two-toned "fee-bee." Can have different calls in different regions. You can see Black-capped Chickadees at roadside pull-offs in both parks. Walk around Fishing Bridge Museum for good looks at these birds.

Mountain Chickadee
Poecile gambeli

YEAR-ROUND
WINTER

Size: 5½" (14 cm)

Male: Overall gray with a black cap, chin and line through the eyes. White eyebrows.

Female: same as male

Juvenile: similar to adult

Nest: cavity, old woodpecker hole or excavates its own; female and male construct; 1-2 broods per year

Eggs: 5-8; white without markings

Incubation: 11-14 days; female and male incubate

Fledging: 18-21 days; female and male feed young

Migration: non-migrator to partial

Food: seeds, insects; visits seed and suet feeders

Compare: The Black-capped Chickadee (pg. 223) is similar, but it lacks the white eyebrows of the Mountain Chickadee.

Stan's Notes: An abundant bird in the state, but more common in coniferous forests in the mountainous regions of Wyoming. Prefers old growth spruce, fir and pine forests. Feeds heavily on coniferous seeds and insects. Flocks with other birds during winter. Moves to lower elevations in winter, returning to high elevations for nesting. Excavates a nest cavity or uses an old woodpecker hole. Will use a nest box. Occasionally uses the same nest site year after year. Lines its nest with moss, hair and feathers. Female will not leave her nest if disturbed, but she will hiss and flutter her wings. Check the trees, especially stands of conifers, at any roadside pull-off in both parks. Mammoth Campground in Yellowstone is always a good place to see this energetic bird.

female
pg. 109

male

pink-sided

Oregon male

Dark-eyed Junco
Junco hyemalis

YEAR-ROUND
WINTER

Size: 5½" (14 cm)

Male: Round, dark-eyed bird with a slate gray-to-charcoal chest, head and back. White belly. Pink bill. Since the outermost tail feathers are white, tail appears as a white V in flight.

Female: same as male, only tan-to-brown color

Juvenile: similar to female, but streaked chest and head

Nest: cup; female and male construct; 2 broods per year

Eggs: 3-5; white with reddish brown markings

Incubation: 12-13 days; female incubates

Fledging: 10-13 days; male and female feed young

Migration: complete to non-migrator in Wyoming

Food: seeds, insects; will come to seed feeders

Compare: Rarely confused with any other bird. Small flocks feed under bird feeders in winter.

Stan's Notes: A year-round bird in Wyoming in higher elevations but usually more commonly seen in winter. Migrates from Canada to Wyoming and beyond. Females tend to fly farther south than the males. Spends the winter in the foothills and plains after snowmelt. Builds nest in a variety of wooded habitats. Adheres to a rigid social hierarchy, with dominant birds chasing the less dominant. Its white outer tail feathers flash when in flight. Often seen in small flocks on the ground, where it will "double-scratch" with both feet simultaneously to expose seeds and insects. Eats many weed seeds. Several junco species were combined into one, simply called Dark-eyed Junco (see lower insets). Pink-sided and Oregon females look nearly identical and are hard to differentiate. Look for all varieties at any time of year in both parks.

male

female

White-breasted Nuthatch
Sitta carolinensis

YEAR-ROUND

Size: 5-6" (13-15 cm)

Male: Slate gray with a white face and belly, and black cap and nape. Long thin bill, slightly upturned. Chestnut undertail.

Female: similar to male, gray cap and nape

Juvenile: similar to female

Nest: cavity; female and male construct; 1 brood per year

Eggs: 5-7; white with brown markings

Incubation: 11-12 days; female incubates

Fledging: 13-14 days; female and male feed young

Migration: non-migrator

Food: insects, seeds; visits seed and suet feeders

Compare: Red-breasted Nuthatch (pg. 221) is smaller with a rust red belly and a distinctive black eye line.

Stan's Notes: The nuthatch's habit of hopping headfirst down tree trunks helps it see insects and insect eggs that birds climbing up the trunk might miss. Incredible climbing agility comes from an extra-long hind toe claw or nail, nearly twice the size of the front toe claws. The name "Nuthatch" comes from the Middle English moniker *nuthak*, referring to the bird's habit of wedging a seed into a crevice and hacking it open. Often seen in flocks with chickadees and Downy Woodpeckers. Mated birds will stay with each other year-round, defending small territories. Listen for its characteristic spring call, "whi-whi-whi-whi," given in February and March. One of 17 worldwide nuthatch species. Look in any stands of larger trees for nuthatches in the parks.

Audubon's male

female

Myrtle male

female

first winter

Yellow-rumped Warbler
Setophaga coronata

MIGRATION
SUMMER

Size: 5-6" (13-15 cm)

Male: Slate gray. Yellow patches on the rump, flanks and head. Two white wing bars. Audubon's has a yellow chin. Myrtle has a white chin.

Female: duller than male, but same yellow patches

Juvenile: similar to female

Nest: cup; female builds; 2 broods per year

Eggs: 4-5; white with brown markings

Incubation: 12-13 days; female incubates

Fledging: 10-12 days; female and male feed young

Migration: complete, to southwestern states, Mexico and Central America

Food: insects, berries; rarely comes to suet feeders

Compare: Male Yellow Warbler (pg. 325) is yellow with orange streaks on its breast. Male Wilson's Warbler (pg. 315) has a black cap. The male Common Yellowthroat (pg. 319) has a yellow chest and distinctive black mask.

Stan's Notes: The two varieties of Yellow-rumped are Audubon's and Myrtle. Audubon's is found in western states and the Myrtle occurs in the eastern U.S., but both are common summer residents and migrators in Wyoming, with flocks of hundreds seen during migration. In winter, the male molts to a dull color similar to the female but retains his yellow patches. Sometimes called Butter-butts due to the yellow patch on the rump. Familiar call is a single robust "chip," heard mostly during migration. Also has a wonderful song in spring.

Say's Phoebe
Sayornis saya

SUMMER

Size: 7½" (19 cm)

Male: Overall dark gray, darkest on head, tail and wings. Belly and undertail tawny. Black bill.

Female: same as male

Juvenile: similar to adult, but browner overall, 2 tawny wing bars and a yellow lower bill

Nest: cup; female builds; 1-2 broods per year

Eggs: 3-6; pale white with brown markings

Incubation: 12-14 days; female incubates

Fledging: 14-16 days; female and male feed young

Migration: complete, to southwestern states, Mexico and Central and South America

Food: insects, berries

Compare: Eastern Kingbird (pg. 237) has a similar size, but it has a white band on the tip of its tail. Townsend's Solitaire (pg. 239) is larger and has a white eye-ring.

Stan's Notes: A widespread bird in Wyoming below 9,000-foot (2,750 m) elevations. Nests in cliff crevices, abandoned buildings, bridges and other vertical structures. Frequently uses the same nest several times in a season, returning the following year to that same nest. A nearly all-insect diet. Flies out from perch to grab an aerial insect and returns to perch (hawking). Also hunts insects on the ground, hovering and dropping down to catch them. Classified as New World Flycatchers and not related to Old World Flycatchers. Named after Thomas Say, who is said to have discovered this bird in Colorado. The genus, species and first part of its common name refer to Mr. Say. "Phoebe" is likely an imitation of the bird's call.

American Dipper
Cinclus mexicanus

YEAR-ROUND

Size: 7½" (19 cm)

Male: Dark gray to black overall; head is slightly lighter in color. A short upturned tail. Dark eyes and bill.

Female: same as male

Juvenile: similar to adult, only paler with white eyelids that are most noticeable when blinking

Nest: pendulous, covered nest with the entrance near the bottom, on a cliff, behind a waterfall; female builds; 1-2 broods per year

Eggs: 3-5; white without markings

Incubation: 13-17 days; female incubates

Fledging: 18-25 days; female and male feed young

Migration: non-migrator; will seek moving open water during winter

Food: aquatic insects, small fish, crustaceans

Compare: Similar shape as American Robin (pg. 247), but lacks a red breast. The only songbird in Wyoming that dives into fast-moving water.

Stan's Notes: A common bird of fast, usually noisy streams that provide some kind of protected shelf on which to construct a nest. Some people have had success attracting dippers with man-made ledges for nesting. Plunges headfirst into fast-moving water, looking for just about any aquatic insect, propelling itself underwater with its wings. Often emerges with a large insect, which it smashes on a rock before eating. Flies directly into the air from underwater. Depending on snowmelt, nesting usually starts in March or April. Dippers in lower elevations often nest two times each year. Look in fast streams in Lamar Valley and the Tower Fall area.

235

Eastern Kingbird
Tyrannus tyrannus

SUMMER

Size: 8" (20 cm)

Male: Mostly black gray bird with a white belly and chin. Black head and tail with a distinctive white band across the end of tail. Red crown is concealed and rarely seen.

Female: same as male

Juvenile: same as adult

Nest: cup; male and female build; 1 brood per year

Eggs: 3-4; white with brown markings

Incubation: 16-18 days; female incubates

Fledging: 16-18 days; female and male feed young

Migration: complete, to Texas, Mexico, Central America and South America

Food: insects, fruit

Compare: The Eastern Kingbird lacks any yellow of the Western Kingbird (pg. 337). Look for a white band on the end of the tail to help identify the Eastern Kingbird.

Stan's Notes: A summer resident seen in open fields. As many as 20 birds migrate together in a group. Returns to the mating ground in spring, where the male and female defend their territory. Acting unafraid of other birds and chasing the larger ones, it is perceived as having an attitude. Its bold behavior gave rise to the common name "King." Perches on tall branches to watch for insects. After flying out to catch them, returns to the same perch–a technique called hawking. Becomes very vocal during late summer, when entire families call back and forth while hunting for insects.

Townsend's Solitaire
Myadestes townsendi

YEAR-ROUND
WINTER

Size: 8½" (22 cm)

Male: All-gray robin look-alike with a prominent white ring around each eye. Wings slightly darker than the body. Long tail. Short dark bill and dark legs.

Female: same as male

Juvenile: darker gray with a tan scaly appearance

Nest: cup; female builds; 1-2 broods per year

Eggs: 3-5; blue, green, gray or white with brown markings

Incubation: 12-14 days; female incubates

Fledging: 10-14 days; female and male feed young

Migration: non-migrator to partial in parts of Wyoming; known to migrate to eastern states

Food: insects, fruit

Compare: American Robin (pg. 247) has a red breast. Clark's Nutcracker (pg. 253) has black wings. Canada Jay (pg. 249) has a white head.

Stan's Notes: A summer resident of coniferous mountain forests, moving lower in winter. "Hawks" for insects, perching in trees and darting out to capture them. Eats berries in winter when insects are unavailable and actively defends a good berry source from other birds. Builds nest on the ground sheltered by rocks or an overhang; sometimes low in a tree or shrub. Song is a series of clear flute-like whistles without a distinct pattern. Shows white outer tail feathers and light tan patches on its wings when in flight. Look in wooded areas above the Upper Terrace, and also the road to Bunsen Peak. Antelope Creek Overlook is another good place to look.

Gray Catbird
Dumetella carolinensis

SUMMER

Size: 9" (22.5 cm)

Male: Handsome slate gray bird with a black crown and long, thin black bill. Often seen with tail lifted up, exposing a chestnut patch beneath the tail.

Female: same as male

Juvenile: same as adult

Nest: cup; female and male construct; 2 broods per year

Eggs: 4-6; blue green without markings

Incubation: 12-13 days; female incubates

Fledging: 10-11 days; female and male feed young

Migration: complete, to southwestern states and Mexico

Food: insects, fruit

Compare: Eastern Kingbird (pg. 237) has a similar size, but it has a white belly and white tail band.

Stan's Notes: A secretive bird. Chippewa Indians gave it a name that means "the bird that cries with grief" due to its raspy call. Call sounds like the mewing of a house cat, hence the common name. Frequently mimics other birds, rarely repeating the same phrases. Found in forests in lower elevations, but it is more often heard than seen. Nests in thick shrubs and quickly flies back into shrubs when approached. If a cowbird introduces an egg into a catbird nest, the catbird will quickly break it, then eject it.

Loggerhead Shrike
Lanius ludovicianus

SUMMER

Size: 9" (22.5 cm)

Male: A gray head and back with black wings and mask across the eyes. White chin, breast and belly. Black tail, legs and feet. Black bill with a hooked tip. White wing patches, as seen during flight.

Female: same as male

Juvenile: dull version of adult

Nest: cup; male and female construct; 1-2 broods per year

Eggs: 4-7; off-white with dark markings

Incubation: 16-17 days; female incubates

Fledging: 17-21 days; female and male feed young

Migration: complete, to southwestern states and Mexico

Food: insects, lizards, small mammals, frogs

Compare: The Cedar Waxwing (pg. 133) has a black mask, but is a brown bird, not gray and black like the Loggerhead Shrike.

Stan's Notes: The Loggerhead is a songbird that acts like a bird of prey. Known for skewering prey on barbed wire fences, thorns and other sharp objects to store or hold still while tearing apart to eat, hence its other common name, Butcher Bird. Feet are too weak to hold the prey it eats. Breeding bird surveys indicate declining populations in the Great Plains due to pesticides killing its major food source–grasshoppers. Look for these birds in open meadows and valleys in both parks.

male

female

Wilson's Phalarope
Phalaropus tricolor

SUMMER

Size: 9¼" (23 cm)

Male: An overall gray bird with a black stripe that runs from the base of bill across the eyes and down the neck. Rusty wash on neck. White chin and sides of body. Long black legs. Thin black bill.

Female: similar to male, but larger and brighter with a more extensive black stripe and rusty wash on front of neck

Juvenile: similar to male, but has yellow legs

Nest: ground; male builds; 1-2 broods per year

Eggs: 3-4; white with brown and black markings

Incubation: 16-21 days; male incubates

Fledging: 8-10 days; male teaches young what to eat

Migration: complete, to South America

Food: small aquatic insects, seeds

Compare: Upland Sandpiper (pg. 153) has a yellow bill. Breeding Spotted Sandpiper (pg. 135) has a speckled white breast and belly. Look for Wilson's Phalarope swimming in tight circles.

Stan's Notes: This unique shorebird is one of the few that swims. The female is often larger and more colorful than the male. Female abandons male after laying eggs, and the male cares for the young. Often swims in tight circles, creating a whirlpool effect that raises aquatic insects to the surface. Picks insects off the water. Unlike other shorebirds, this one has lobed toes. Often seen alone or in small groups. Often feeds with American Avocets in shallow water. One of three phalarope species in North America and the only one that breeds south of Canada and Alaska.

male

female

American Robin
Turdus migratorius

YEAR-ROUND
SUMMER

Size: 9-11" (22.5-28 cm)

Male: A familiar gray bird with a rusty red breast and nearly black head and tail. White chin with black streaks. White eye-ring.

Female: similar to male, but with a gray head and a duller breast

Juvenile: similar to female, but has a speckled breast and brown back

Nest: cup; female builds with help from the male; 2-3 broods per year

Eggs: 4-7; pale blue without markings

Incubation: 12-14 days; female incubates

Fledging: 14-16 days; female and male feed young

Migration: complete to non-migrator in Wyoming

Food: insects, fruit, berries, earthworms

Compare: Familiar bird to all.

Stan's Notes: The robin is a complete migrator in high elevations, but it's also a year-round resident in parts of Wyoming. Some of the birds don't migrate, spending the winter in low areas, feeding on leftover berries and insect eggs. Can be heard singing all night in spring. Many people do not realize how easy it is to differentiate between male and female robins. Compare the male's dark, nearly black head and brick red breast with the female's gray head and dull red breast. A robin is not listening for worms moving when cocking its head to one side. It is looking at the earth with its eyes, which are placed far back on the sides of its head. Very territorial, often fighting its own reflection in windows. Commonly seen in both parks at all elevations during summer.

Canada Jay
Perisoreus canadensis

YEAR-ROUND

Size: 11½" (29 cm)

Male: Large gray bird with a white forehead and nape of neck. Short black bill. Dark eyes.

Female: same as male

Juvenile: sooty gray with a faint white whisker mark

Nest: cup; male and female build; 1 brood per year

Eggs: 3-4; gray white, finely marked to unmarked

Incubation: 16-18 days; female incubates

Fledging: 14-15 days; male and female feed young

Migration: non-migrator

Food: insects, seeds, fruit, nuts; visits seed feeders

Compare: Slightly larger than the Pinyon Jay (pg. 95) and Steller's Jay (pg. 97), but lacks the blue coloring. The Clark's Nutcracker (pg. 253) is slightly larger with black wings.

Stan's Notes: A bird of coniferous woods, found in mid to high elevations. Known as Camp Robber because it rummages through camps looking for scraps of food. Also called Whiskey Jack or Gray Jay. Easily tamed, this bird will fly to your hand if offered raisins or nuts. Will eat just about anything. Also stores extra food for the winter, balling it together in a sticky mass, placing it on a tree branch, often concealing it with lichen or bark. Travels around in small family units of 3-5, making good companions for campers and high-altitude hikers and climbers. Reminds some people of an overgrown chickadee. Check the conifers near LeHardy Rapids in Yellowstone, and the picnic area near Scaup Lake in the southwest part of the park. Many roadside pull-offs have friendly Canada Jays. Most campgrounds in the Tetons also have these birds.

soaring

juvenile

Sharp-shinned Hawk
Accipiter striatus

YEAR-ROUND
WINTER

Size: 10-14" (25-36 cm); up to 2-foot wingspan

Male: Small woodland hawk with a gray back and head and rusty red chest. The tail is long with several dark tail bands; widest band is at the end of tail, which is squared. Red eyes.

Female: same as male, only larger

Juvenile: same size as adults, with a brown back and heavily streaked breast, yellow eyes

Nest: platform; female builds; 1 brood per year

Eggs: 4-5; white with brown markings

Incubation: 32-35 days; female incubates

Fledging: 24-27 days; female and male feed young

Migration: non-migrator to partial in Wyoming

Food: birds, small mammals

Compare: Cooper's Hawk (pg. 261) is very similar, but larger, with a larger head, slightly longer neck and rounded tail. Look for the squared tail of Sharp-shinned Hawk to help identify.

Stan's Notes: Common hawk of backyards and woodlands, often seen swooping in on birds visiting feeders. Its short, rounded wings and long tail allow it to navigate through thick stands of trees in pursuit of prey. Common name comes from the sharp keel on the leading edge of the "shin," although this is actually below (rather than above) the bird's ankle on the tarsus bone of the foot. In most birds, the tarsus is round. In flight, the head doesn't protrude as far as that of the Cooper's Hawk.

Clark's Nutcracker
Nucifraga columbiana

YEAR-ROUND

Size: 12" (30 cm)

Male: Gray with black wings and a narrow black band down the center of tail. Small white patches on long wings, seen in flight. Has a relatively short tail with a white undertail.

Female: same as male

Juvenile: same as adult

Nest: cup; female and male build; 1 brood per year

Eggs: 2-5; pale green with brown markings

Incubation: 16-18 days; female and male incubate

Fledging: 18-20 days; female and male feed young

Migration: non-migrator

Food: seeds, insects, berries, eggs, mammals

Compare: Canada Jay (pg. 249) lacks the black wings of Nutcracker. Townsend's Solitaire (pg. 239) is smaller, lacks black wings and has a smaller bill. The Steller's Jay (pg. 97) is dark blue with a black crest.

Stan's Notes: A high country bird in coniferous forests in the state. Diet varies, but it relies heavily on piñon seeds, often caching large quantities to eat later or feed to its young. Uses the large pouch in its throat (sublingual pouch) to transport seeds. Studies show that these birds can carry up to 100 seeds at a time. Nests early in the year, often while snow still covers the ground, relying on stored foods. A "Lewis and Clark" bird, first recorded in Idaho by William Clark in 1805. Seen at high elevation roadside pull-outs, such as Dunraven Pass. Sylvan Pass to the East Entrance is also a good place to check, as well as around the Lewis Canyon rim.

Eurasian Collared-Dove
Streptopelia decaocto

Size: 12½" (32 cm)

Male: Head, neck, chest and belly are pale gray to light tan. A slightly darker back, wings and tail. Black collar with a white border extends around nape of neck. Long squared-off tail.

Female: same as male

Juvenile: similar to adult

Nest: platform; female and male build; 2-3 broods per year

Eggs: 3-5; creamy white without markings

Incubation: 12-14 days; female and male incubate

Fledging: 12-14 days; female and male feed young

Migration: non-migrator

Food: seeds

Compare: Slightly larger and lighter in color than the Mourning Dove (pg. 157). Look for a black collar and squared tail to help identify.

Stan's Notes: A non-native bird found only at low elevations. Moved into Florida in the 1980s after introduction to the Bahamas; reached northern and western states in the late 1990s. It has been expanding its range across North America and is predicted to spread here the same way it did through Europe from Asia. Unknown how this "new" bird will affect the native Mourning Dove. Nearly identical to the Ringed Turtle-Dove, a common pet bird species.

Rock Pigeon
Columba livia

YEAR-ROUND

Size: 13" (33 cm)

Male: No set color pattern. Gray to white, patches of iridescent greens and blues, usually with a light rump patch.

Female: same as male

Juvenile: same as adult

Nest: platform; female builds; 3-4 broods per year

Eggs: 1-2; white without markings

Incubation: 18-20 days; female and male incubate

Fledging: 25-26 days; female and male feed young

Migration: non-migrator

Food: seeds; will visit feeders

Compare: Eurasian Collared-Dove (pg. 255) has a black collar. Mourning Dove (pg. 157) is smaller, light brown and lacks all the color variations of the Rock Pigeon.

Stan's Notes: Also known as Domestic Pigeon, formerly known as Rock Dove. Introduced to North America from Europe by the early settlers. Most common around cities and barnyards, where it scratches for seeds. One of the few birds with a wide variety of colors, produced by years of selective breeding while in captivity. Parents feed the young a regurgitated liquid known as crop-milk for the first few days of life. One of the few birds that can drink without tilting its head back. Builds nest underneath bridges and on buildings, balconies, barns and sheds. Was once poisoned as a "nuisance city bird." Many cities now have Peregrine Falcons (not shown), which feed on the pigeons, keeping their numbers in check.

winter

in flight

breeding

Franklin's Gull
Leucophaeus pipixcan

MIGRATION
SUMMER

Size: 14-15" (36-38 cm); up to 3-foot wingspan

Male: Gray and white plumage with a black head and black extending partially down the neck. Black wing tips. Large white eye-ring. Reddish bill. Winter plumage has a partial black "hood" and black bill.

Female: same as male

Juvenile: brown back, black bill, lacks all-black head

Nest: floating platform; male and female construct; 1 brood per year

Eggs: 2-4; greenish with brown markings

Incubation: 24-25 days; female and male incubate

Fledging: 31-33 days; female and male feed young

Migration: complete, to southwestern states, Mexico and Central and South America

Food: insects, fish

Compare: Regularly occurring black-headed gull in Wyoming. Look for it in open marshes, with its black "hood" and black wing tips. Ring-billed Gull (pg. 307) is larger and lacks the black head of the breeding Franklin's.

Stan's Notes: Most common during migration, when hundreds gather in lakes. A three-year gull, young obtain adult plumage at 3 years of age. Juveniles are brown with partially black heads. The first- and second-year birds are like winter adults, with gray and white plumage, partially black heads and black bills. The breeding range is from Minnesota and the Dakotas west to Wyoming and Montana and north into Canada.

soaring

juvenile

Cooper's Hawk
Accipiter cooperii

YEAR-ROUND
SUMMER

Size: 14-20" (36-50 cm); up to 3-foot wingspan

Male: Medium-sized hawk with short wings and a long rounded tail with several black bands. Rusty breast and dark wing tips. Slate gray back. Bright yellow spot at base of gray bill (cere). Dark red eyes.

Female: similar to male, only slightly larger

Juvenile: brown back with brown streaks on breast, bright yellow eyes

Nest: platform; male and female construct; 1 brood per year

Eggs: 2-4; greenish with brown markings

Incubation: 32-36 days; female and male incubate

Fledging: 28-32 days; male and female feed young

Migration: non-migrator to partial in Wyoming

Food: small birds, mammals

Compare: Nearly identical to the Sharp-shinned Hawk (pg. 251), only it is larger, darker gray and has a rounded tail.

Stan's Notes: A common resident hawk of woodlands. During flight, look for its large head, short wings and long tail. The stubby wings help it maneuver between trees while pursuing small birds. Comes to feeders, hunting for unaware birds. Flies with long glides followed by a few quick flaps. Known to ambush prey, flying into heavy brush or even running on the ground in pursuit. Nestlings have gray eyes that become bright yellow at 1 year of age and turn dark red later, after 3-5 years.

female
pg. 197

male

soaring

Northern Harrier
Circus hudsonius

YEAR-ROUND

Size: 18-22" (45-56 cm); up to 4-foot wingspan

Male: A slim, low-flying hawk. Silver gray with a large white rump patch and a white belly. Faint narrow bands across tail. Black wing tips. Yellow eyes.

Female: dark brown back, brown-streaked breast and belly, large white rump patch, narrow black bands across tail, black wing tips, yellow eyes

Juvenile: similar to female, with an orange chest

Nest: ground; female and male construct; 1 brood per year

Eggs: 4-8; bluish white without markings

Incubation: 31-32 days; female incubates

Fledging: 30-35 days; male and female feed young

Migration: non-migrator to partial in Wyoming

Food: mice, snakes, insects, small birds

Compare: Slimmer than the Red-tailed Hawk (pg. 203). Look for black tail bands, a white rump patch and the characteristic flight to help identify.

Stan's Notes: One of the easiest of hawks to identify. Glides near the ground, following the contours of the land while searching for prey. Holds its wings just above a horizontal position, tilting back and forth in the wind, similar to Turkey Vultures. Formerly called Marsh Hawk due to its habit of hunting over marshes. Feeds on the ground. Will perch on the ground to preen and rest. Unlike other hawks, uses its hearing primarily to locate prey, followed by eyesight. At any age, it has a distinctive owl-like face disk. Look for it in Hayden and Lamar Valleys in Yellowstone. Also along the road just outside Jenny Lake Campground in the Tetons.

non-displaying

female
pg. 181

displaying male

Dusky Grouse
Dendragapus obscurus

YEAR-ROUND

Size: 19" (48 cm)

Male: Dark gray chicken-like bird. Bright yellow-to-orange patch of skin above the eyes (comb). Shows white feathers surrounding an inflated purplish sac on neck when displaying. Fans a gray-tipped, nearly black tail.

Female: mottled brown bird, gray belly, yellow patch of skin above eyes (comb)

Juvenile: similar to female

Nest: ground; female builds; 1 brood per year

Eggs: 6-12; pale white with brown markings

Incubation: 24-26 days; female incubates

Fledging: 7-10 days; female feeds young

Migration: non-migrator; will move around to find food

Food: insects, seeds, fruit, leaf buds and coniferous needles (Douglas-fir)

Compare: Larger than Ruffed Grouse (pg. 179). Look for the male's obvious yellow-to-orange comb.

Stan's Notes: The most common grouse of the Rockies, found from the foothills to the timberline. Usually on the ground but also in trees during spring, feeding on newly opened leaf buds. Often switches from an insect diet in summer to coniferous needles in winter. Male engages in elaborate courtship displays by fanning its tail, inflating its bright neck sac and singing (calling). Male mates with several females. Young leave the nest within 24 hours after hatching and follow their mothers to feed. Very tame and freezes if threatened, making it easy to get a close look. Hike trails, wooded ridges and mid-elevations in the parks to see this bird.

female pg. 191

male

Gadwall
Mareca strepera

YEAR-ROUND
SUMMER

Size: 20" (50 cm)

Male: A plump gray duck with a brown head and a distinctive black rump. White belly and chestnut-tinged wings. Bright white wing linings. Small white wing patch, seen when swimming. Gray bill.

Female: similar to female Mallard, a mottled brown with a pronounced color change from a dark brown body to a light brown neck and head, bright white wing linings, small white wing patch and gray bill with orange sides

Juvenile: similar to female

Nest: ground; female lines the nest with fine grass and down feathers plucked from her breast; 1 brood per year

Eggs: 8-11; white without markings

Incubation: 24-27 days; female incubates

Fledging: 48-56 days; young feed themselves

Migration: complete to non-migrator in Wyoming

Food: aquatic insects

Compare: Male Gadwall is one of the few gray ducks. Look for its distinctive black rump.

Stan's Notes: A duck of shallow marshes. Consumes mostly plant material, dunking its head in water to feed rather than tipping forward, like other dabbling ducks. Walks well on land; feeds in fields and woodlands. Frequently in pairs with other duck species. Nests within 300 feet (100 m) of water. Establishes pair bond in winter.

in flight

Canada Goose
Branta canadensis

YEAR-ROUND

Size: 25-43" (63-109 cm); up to 5½-foot wingspan

Male: Large gray goose with a black neck and head and a white chin or cheek strap.

Female: same as male

Juvenile: same as adult

Nest: platform, on the ground; female constructs; 1 brood per year

Eggs: 5-10; white without markings

Incubation: 25-30 days; female incubates

Fledging: 42-55 days; male and female teach the young to feed

Migration: non-migrator to partial; moves around to find open water in winter

Food: aquatic plants, insects, seeds

Compare: Large goose, rarely confused with other birds.

Stan's Notes: A common bird year-round in Wyoming. Formerly killed off (extirpated) in many areas, it was reintroduced and now is common. Begins breeding in the third year, and adults mate for many years. Males frequently act as sentinels, standing at the edge of their group, bobbing their heads up and down, and becoming extremely aggressive to anyone who approaches. Will hiss as though displaying displeasure. Adults molt their primary flight feathers while raising the young, rendering family groups flightless at the same time. Several subspecies vary geographically across the United States; generally they're darker in western groups and paler in the East. Size decreases northward, with the smallest subspecies seen on the Arctic tundra. Commonly seen nesting in both parks.

in flight

rusty stain

rusty stain
in flight

Sandhill Crane
Antigone canadensis

MIGRATION
SUMMER

Size: 40-48" (102-120 cm); up to 7-foot wingspan

Male: Elegant gray bird with long legs and neck. Wings and body often stained rusty brown. Scarlet red cap. Yellow-to-red eyes.

Female: same as male

Juvenile: dull brown, lacks red cap, has yellow eyes

Nest: platform, on the ground; female and male build; 1 brood per year

Eggs: 2; olive with brown markings

Incubation: 28-32 days; female and male incubate

Fledging: 65 days; female and male feed young

Migration: complete, to southwestern states and Mexico

Food: insects, fruit, worms, plants, amphibians

Compare: Similar size as Great Blue Heron (pg. 273), but the Sandhill has a shorter bill and a red cap. The Great Blue Heron holds its neck in an S shape during flight unlike the Sandhill's straight neck in flight. Look for the scarlet red cap to help identify the Sandhill Crane.

Stan's Notes: Among the tallest birds in the world and capable of flying at great heights. Usually seen in large undisturbed fields near water. Has a very distinctive rattling call. Often heard before seen. Plumage often looks rusty brown (see insets) due to staining from mud during preening. A characteristic flight with upstroke quicker than down. Performing a spectacular mating dance, the birds face each other, bow and jump into the air while uttering loud cackling sounds and flapping wings. Often flips sticks and grass into the air during the dance. Once uncommon in the parks, now nests in both. Look at Wildlife Overlook at Fountain Flats.

in flight

Great Blue Heron
Ardea herodias

YEAR-ROUND
MIGRATION
SUMMER

Size: 42-52" (107-132 cm); up to 6-foot wingspan

Male: Tall gray heron. Black eyebrows extend into several long plumes off the back of head. Long yellow bill. Feathers at the base of neck drop down in a kind of necklace.

Female: same as male

Juvenile: same as adult, but more brown than gray, a black crown and lacks plumes

Nest: platform; male and female construct; 1 brood per year

Eggs: 3-5; blue green without markings

Incubation: 27-28 days; female and male incubate

Fledging: 56-60 days; male and female feed young

Migration: complete to non-migrator in Wyoming

Food: small fish, frogs, insects, snakes

Compare: Similar size as Sandhill Crane (pg. 271), but lacks the red crown. Sandhill flies holding its neck straight unlike the Great Blue's S-shaped neck. Look for the long neck and yellow bill of Great Blue Heron to help identify.

Stan's Notes: One of the most common herons, often barking like a dog when startled. Stalks small fish in shallow water. Strikes at mice, squirrels and just about anything else it may come across. Holds neck in an S shape in flight with its long legs trailing straight out behind, and holds wings in a cupped fashion. Nests in colonies of up to 100 birds. Nests in treetops near or over open water. A few may remain in winter where they can find open water.

male

female

Calliope Hummingbird

Selasphorus calliope

MIGRATION
SUMMER

Size: 3¼" (8 cm)

Male: Iridescent green head, back and tail. Breast and belly white to tan. V-shaped iridescent rosy red throat patch (gorget). A very short, thin bill and short tail compared with other hummingbirds. Wing tips reach to tip of tail.

Female: same as male, but thin, spotty throat patch

Juvenile: similar to female

Nest: cup; female builds; 1 brood per year

Eggs: 1-2; white without markings

Incubation: 15-17 days; female incubates

Fledging: 18-22 days; female feeds young

Migration: complete, to Central and South America

Food: nectar, insects; will come to nectar feeders

Compare: The Broad-tailed Hummingbird (pg. 277) is very similar with a longer tail, which extends beyond its wing tips when perched. Look for a short thin bill, short tail and wing tips extending past the tail when perched.

Stan's Notes: Smallest bird in North America. A relatively quiet bird that will come to nectar feeders. During the breeding season, males can be heard zinging around while displaying for females. Females are hard to distinguish from other female hummingbirds. Often builds nest on branches of pine trees. Juvenile males obtain a partial throat patch by fall of their first year. Look in flower-filled meadows at middle to high elevations in both parks.

male

female

Broad-tailed Hummingbird
Selasphorus platycercus

MIGRATION
SUMMER

Size: 4" (10 cm)

Male: Tiny iridescent green bird with a black throat patch (gorget) reflect rosy red in sunlight. Wings and part of back green. White chest.

Female: same as male, but lacking the throat patch, much more green on back, tan flanks

Juvenile: similar to female

Nest: cup; female builds; 1-2 broods per year

Eggs: 1-3; white without markings

Incubation: 12-14 days; female incubates

Fledging: 20-22 days; female feeds young

Migration: complete, to Central and South America

Food: nectar, insects; will come to nectar feeders

Compare: Calliope Hummingbird (pg. 275) is smaller and has wing tips that reach to the tip of its tail when perched.

Stan's Notes: Hummingbirds are the only birds with the ability to fly backward. Does not sing. Will chatter or buzz to communicate. Wing beats produce a whistle, almost like a tiny ringing bell. Heart pumps an incredible 1,260 beats every minute. Weighing just 2-3 grams, it takes about five average-sized hummingbirds to equal the weight of one chickadee. Male performs a spectacular pendulum-like flight over the perched female. After mating, female builds the nest and raises young without any help from her mate. Constructs a soft, flexible nest that expands to accommodate the growing young. High meadows in both parks will have Broad-tails.

male

female

Violet-green Swallow
Tachycineta thalassina

SUMMER

Size: 5¼" (13.5 cm)

Male: Dull emerald green crown, nape and back. Violet blue wings and tail. White chest and belly. White cheeks with white extending above the eyes. Wings extend beyond the tail when perching.

Female: same as male, only duller

Juvenile: similar to adult of the same sex

Nest: cavity; female and male build nest in tree cavities, old woodpecker holes; 1 brood per year

Eggs: 4-6; pale white with brown markings

Incubation: 13-14 days; female incubates

Fledging: 18-24 days; female and male feed young

Migration: complete, to Central and South America

Food: insects

Compare: Similar size as Cliff Swallow (pg. 113), which has a distinctive tan-to-rust pattern on its head. Barn Swallow (pg. 89) has a distinctive, deeply forked tail. The Tree Swallow (pg. 87) is mostly deep blue, lacking any emerald green of the Violet-green Swallow.

Stan's Notes: A solitary nester in tree cavities and rarely beneath cliff overhangs, unlike the colony-nesting Cliff Swallows. Like Tree Swallows, can be attracted with a nest box. Will search for miles for errant feathers to line its nest. Tail is short and wing tips extend beyond the end of it, seen when perching. Returns to Wyoming in April; begins nesting in May. Young often leave the nest by June. Look around the edges of aspen groves in the parks, where these swallows are nesting in old woodpecker holes.

Green-tailed Towhee
Pipilo chlorurus

MIGRATION
SUMMER

Size: 7¼" (18.5 cm)

Male: Unique yellowish green back, wings and tail. Dark gray chest and face. Bright white throat with black stripes. Rusty red crown.

Female: same as male

Juvenile: olive green with heavy streaking on chest and belly, lacks a crown and throat markings

Nest: cup; female and male construct; 1-2 broods per year

Eggs: 3-5; white with brown markings

Incubation: 12-14 days; female and male incubate

Fledging: 10-14 days; female and male feed young

Migration: complete, to southwestern states, Mexico and Central America

Food: insects, seeds, fruit; will visit feeders

Compare: The male Spotted Towhee (pg. 29) is black and has rusty sides. The unusual color of the Green-tailed, along with its short wings, long tail and large bill, make it easy to identify.

Stan's Notes: A common bird of shrubby hillsides and sagebrush mountain slopes up to 7,000 feet (2,150 m). Like other towhee species, searches for insects and seeds, taking a little jump forward while kicking backward with both feet. Known for scurrying away from trouble by jumping to the ground without opening its wings and then running across the ground. Arrives in Wyoming in April. Begins breeding in May.

Lewis's Woodpecker
Melanerpes lewis

YEAR-ROUND
MIGRATION

Size: 10¾" (27.5 cm)

Male: Dull green head and back. Distinctive gray collar and breast. Deep red face and a light red belly.

Female: same as male

Juvenile: similar to adult, with a brown head, lacking the red face

Nest: cavity; male and female excavate; 1 brood per year

Eggs: 4-8; white without markings

Incubation: 13-14 days; female and male incubate

Fledging: 28-34 days; female and male feed young

Migration: non-migrator to partial; moves around to find food in winter

Food: insects, nuts, seeds, berries

Compare: Male Williamson's Sapsucker (pg. 59) has a black back and large white wing patches. The Red-naped Sapsucker (pg. 57) has a black-and white pattern on its back and much more red on its head.

Stan's Notes: Large and handsome woodpecker of western states. First collected and named in 1805 by Lewis and Clark in Montana. During breeding season, it feeds exclusively on insects rather than grubs, like other woodpeckers. Prefers open pine forests and areas with recent forest fires. Excavates in dead or soft wood. Uses the same cavity year after year. Tends to mate for the long term. Moves around during winter to search for food such as pine nuts (seeds). Uncommon in both parks.

female pg. 189

male

Northern Shoveler
Spatula clypeata

SUMMER

Size:	20" (50 cm)
Male:	Medium-sized duck with an iridescent green head, rusty sides and white breast. An extraordinarily large, spoon-shaped bill that is almost always held pointed toward the water.
Female:	brown and black all over, green speculum, spoon-shaped bill
Juvenile:	same as female
Nest:	ground; female builds; 1 brood per year
Eggs:	9-12; olive without markings
Incubation:	22-25 days; female incubates
Fledging:	30-60 days; female leads young to food
Migration:	complete, to southwestern states, Mexico and Central America
Food:	aquatic insects, plants
Compare:	Similar to male Mallard (pg. 287), but male Northern Shoveler has a large, characteristic spoon-shaped bill.

Stan's Notes: Named for the peculiar shape of the bill. "Northern" in the common name was given because this is the only species of these ducks in North America. Found in small flocks of 5-10 birds, swimming low in water, pointing its large bill toward the water as if it's too heavy to lift. Feeds mainly by filtering tiny aquatic insects and plants from the water's surface with its bill, often swimming in tight circles while feeding. Check all large and small lakes in both parks for shovelers.

female pg. 187

male

Mallard
Anas platyrhynchos

YEAR-ROUND

Size: 19-21" (48-53 cm)

Male: A large, bulbous green head, white necklace and rust brown or chestnut chest. Gray and white on the sides. Yellow bill. Orange legs and feet.

Female: brown duck with an orange and black bill and blue and white wing mark (speculum)

Juvenile: same as female, but with a yellow bill

Nest: ground; female builds; 1 brood per year

Eggs: 7-10; greenish to whitish, unmarked

Incubation: 26-30 days; female incubates

Fledging: 42-52 days; female leads young to food

Migration: partial to non-migrator in Wyoming; moves around to find open water and food in winter

Food: seeds, plants, aquatic insects; will come to ground feeders offering corn

Compare: Most people recognize this common duck. The male Northern Shoveler (pg. 285) has a white breast with rust on the sides and a large spoon-shaped bill.

Stan's Notes: A familiar duck of lakes and ponds, it's considered a type of dabbling duck, tipping forward in shallow water to feed on aquatic plants on the bottom. The name "Mallard" comes from the Latin *masculus*, meaning "male," referring to the habit of males not taking part in raising ducklings. Black central tail feathers of male curl upward. Both the male and female have white tails and white underwings. Will return to place of birth.

in flight

female pg. 305

male

Common Merganser
Mergus merganser

YEAR-ROUND
MIGRATION
WINTER

Size: 27" (69 cm)

Male: Long, thin, duck-like bird with a green head, black back, and white sides, chest and neck. A long, pointed orange bill. Often appears to be black and white in poor light.

Female: same size and shape as the male, but has a rusty red head with ragged "hair" and a gray body with white chest and chin

Juvenile: same as female

Nest: cavity; female lines an old woodpecker cavity; 1 brood per year

Eggs: 9-11; ivory without markings

Incubation: 28-33 days; female incubates

Fledging: 70-80 days; female feeds young

Migration: non-migrator to partial in Wyoming; moves around to find open water

Food: small fish, aquatic insects

Compare: Male Mallard (pg. 287) is smaller and lacks the black back and long pointed bill.

Stan's Notes: Can be seen on just about any open water during the winter, but more common along large rivers than lakes. This is a shallow water diver that feeds on fish in 10-15 feet (3-4.5 m) of water. The bill has a fine, serrated-like edge to help catch slippery fish. Females often lay their eggs in nests of other mergansers (egg dumping), resulting in broods of up to 15 young per mother. Male leaves the female as soon as she starts to incubate eggs. Orphans are accepted by other merganser mothers with young. Flies back and forth between large rivers and lakes, so check Fishing Bridge and Pelican Bridge in Yellowstone.

289

female
pg. 321

male

American Redstart
Setophaga ruticilla

MIGRATION
SUMMER

Size: 5" (13 cm)

Male: A small, striking black bird with contrasting patches of orange on sides, wings and tail. White belly.

Female: olive brown with yellow patches on sides, wings and tail, white belly

Juvenile: same as female, juvenile male attains orange tinges in the second year

Nest: cup; female builds; 1 brood per year

Eggs: 3-5; off-white with brown markings

Incubation: 12 days; female incubates

Fledging: 9 days; female and male feed young

Migration: complete, to Mexico, Central America and South America

Food: insects, seeds, berries rarely

Compare: The male Red-winged Blackbird (pg. 31) is much larger at roughly 8 inches (20 cm). The only small black and orange bird flitting around the top of trees.

Stan's Notes: A common and widespread warbler throughout Wyoming during migration and summer. Prefers large, unbroken tracts of forest. Appears to be hyperactive when feeding, hovering and darting back and forth to glean insects from leaves. Often droops its wings and fans tail just before launching out to catch an insect. Look for the male's flashing black and orange colors high up in trees.

female pg. 333

male

Bullock's Oriole
Icterus bullockii

SUMMER

Size: 8" (20 cm)

Male: Bright orange and black bird. Black crown, eye line, nape, chin, wings and back contrast with the orange plumage and the bold white patch on the wings.

Female: dull yellow overall with a pale white belly and white wing bars on gray-to-black wings

Juvenile: similar to female

Nest: pendulous; female and male build; 1 brood per year

Eggs: 4-6; pale white to gray with brown markings

Incubation: 12-14 days; female incubates

Fledging: 12-14 days; female and male feed young

Migration: complete, to Central and South America

Food: insects, berries, nectar; visits nectar feeders

Compare: A handsome bird. Same size as male Black-headed Grosbeak (pg. 295), which has more black on its head and a short, thick bicolored bill. Look for the bright markings and a thin black line running through each eye of the male Bullock's Oriole.

Stan's Notes: So closely related to Baltimore Orioles of the eastern U.S., at one time both were considered one species. Interbreeds with Baltimores where ranges overlap. Most common in Wyoming where cottonwood trees grow along rivers and other wetlands. Also seen at the edge of clearings, in city parks, on farms and along irrigation ditches. Builds a hanging sock-like nest with plant fibers such as the inner bark of junipers and willows. Will incorporate yarn and thread into the nest if offered during nest building.

female
pg. 137

male

Black-headed Grosbeak
Pheucticus melanocephalus

SUMMER

Size: 8" (20 cm)

Male: Stocky bird with a burnt orange breast, neck and rump. Black head, tail and wings with irregular-shaped white wing patches. A large bill with upper bill darker than the lower.

Female: appears like a large sparrow, overall brown, lighter breast and belly, large two-toned bill, bold white eyebrows, yellow wing linings

Juvenile: similar to adult of the same sex

Nest: cup; female builds; 1 brood per year

Eggs: 3-4; pale green or bluish with brown marks

Incubation: 11-13 days; female and male incubate

Fledging: 11-13 days; female and male feed young

Migration: complete, to Mexico, Central America and northern South America

Food: seeds, insects, fruit; comes to seed feeders

Compare: Male Evening Grosbeak (pg. 335) is the same size, but the male Black-headed has an orange breast and lacks the yellow belly. Male Bullock's Oriole (pg. 293) has more white on the wings than the male Black-headed. Look for the bicolored large, thick bill.

Stan's Notes: A bird that nests in a wide variety of habitats, but seems to prefer the foothills slightly more than other places. Both males and females sing and aggressively defend their nests against intruders. Song is very similar to the American Robin's and Western Tanager's, making it hard to tell them apart by song. Populations are increasing in Wyoming and across the U.S.

male

female
pg. 105

yellow
male

House Finch
Haemorhous mexicanus

YEAR-ROUND

Size: 5" (13 cm)

Male: An orange red face, breast and rump, with a brown cap. Brown marking behind the eyes. Brown wings streaked with white. A white belly with brown streaks.

Female: brown with a heavily streaked white chest

Juvenile: similar to female

Nest: cup, occasionally in a cavity, female builds; 2 broods per year

Eggs: 4-5; pale blue, lightly marked

Incubation: 12-14 days; female incubates

Fledging: 15-19 days; female and male feed young

Migration: non-migrator to partial; will move around to find food

Food: seeds, fruit, leaf buds; will visit seed feeders

Compare: Smaller than male Red Crossbill (pg. 299), which has a large crossed bill. Look for brown streaks on the belly to help identify the male House Finch.

Stan's Notes: Very social, visiting feeders in small flocks. Can be the most common bird at feeders. Likes to nest in hanging flower baskets. Male sings a loud, cheerful warbling song. Historically it occurred from the Pacific Coast to the Rocky Mountains, with a few reaching the eastern side. Birds introduced to Long Island, New York, in the 1940s have populated the entire eastern U.S. Now found throughout the U.S. Male feeds the incubating female. Suffers from a fatal eye disease that causes the eyes to crust. Rarely, some males are yellow (see inset), probably due to poor diet.

female
pg. 327

male

Red Crossbill
Loxia curvirostra

YEAR-ROUND

Size: 6½" (16 cm)

Male: Sparrow-sized bird, dirty red to orange with a bright red crown and rump. Dark brown wings. Short dark brown tail. Long, pointed crossed bill.

Female: pale yellow breast, light gray throat patch, a crossed bill, dark brown wings and tail

Juvenile: streaked with tinges of yellow, bill gradually crosses about 2 weeks after fledging

Nest: cup; female builds; 1 brood per year

Eggs: 3-4; bluish white with brown markings

Incubation: 14-18 days; female incubates

Fledging: 16-20 days; female and male feed young

Migration: non-migrator to irruptive; moves around the state in winter to find food; will wander as far south as Mexico

Food: seeds, leaf buds; comes to seed feeders

Compare: Larger than the male House Finch (pg. 297), which lacks the dark brown wings. Look for the unique crossed bill to help identify.

Stan's Notes: The long crossed bill is adapted for extracting seeds from pine and spruce cones, its favorite food. Often dangles upside down like a parrot to reach cones. Also seen on the ground where it eats grit, which helps digest food. Nests in coniferous forests. Some studies show up to nine distinct populations of Red Crossbills, but they are nearly impossible to distinguish in the field. Plumage can be highly variable among individuals. Irruptive behavior makes it more common in some winters and nonexistent in others.

female pg. 183

male

Redhead
Aythya americana

MIGRATION
SUMMER

Size: 19" (48 cm)

Male: Rich red head and neck with a black breast and tail. Gray sides. Smoky gray wings and back. Tricolored bill with a light blue base, white ring and black tip.

Female: soft brown plain-looking duck with gray-to-white wing linings, rounded top of head and gray bill with a black tip

Juvenile: similar to female

Nest: cup; female builds; 1 brood per year

Eggs: 9-14; pale white without markings

Incubation: 24-28 days; female and male incubate

Fledging: 56-73 days; female shows young what to eat

Migration: complete, to southwestern states, Mexico and Central America

Food: seeds, aquatic plants, insects

Compare: Male Northern Shoveler (pg. 285) has a green head and rusty sides unlike the red head and gray sides of the male Redhead.

Stan's Notes: A duck of permanent large bodies of water. Forages along the shoreline, feeding on seeds, aquatic plants and insects. Usually builds nest directly on the water's surface, using large mats of vegetation. Female lays up to 75 percent of its eggs in the nests of other Redheads and several other duck species. Nests primarily in the Prairie Pothole region of the northern Great Plains. Overall populations seem to be increasing at about 2-3 percent each year.

female pg. 195

male

Canvasback
Aythya valisineria

MIGRATION
SUMMER

Size: 20½" (52 cm)

Male: Deep red head with a sloping forehead that transitions into a long black bill. Red neck. Gray and white sides and back. Black chest and tail.

Female: similar to male, but has a brown head, neck and breast, light gray-to-brown sides and a long dark bill

Juvenile: similar to female

Nest: ground; female builds; 1 brood per year

Eggs: 7-9; pale white to gray without markings

Incubation: 24-29 days; female incubates

Fledging: 56-67 days; female leads young to food

Migration: complete, to southwestern states and Mexico

Food: aquatic insects, small clams

Compare: The male Lesser Scaup (pg. 69) is smaller, has a shorter, light-colored bill and lacks the red head and neck of the male Canvasback.

Stan's Notes: A large inland duck of freshwater lakes, rivers and ponds. Populations declined dramatically in the 1960-80s due to marsh drainage for agriculture. Females return to their birthplace (philopatric) while males disperse to new areas. Will mate during migration or on the breeding grounds. A courting male gives a soft cooing call when displaying and during aerial chases. Male leaves the female after incubation starts. Female takes a new mate every year. Female feeds very little during incubation and will lose up to 70 percent of fat reserves during that time. Yellowstone Lake and Jackson Lake are popular places to look for this waterfowl.

in flight

male pg. 289

female

Common Merganser

Mergus merganser

YEAR-ROUND
MIGRATION
WINTER

Size: 27" (69 cm)

Female: A long, thin, duck-like bird with a rusty red head and ragged "hair" on the back of head. Gray body with white chest and chin. Long, pointed orange bill.

Male: same size and shape as the female, but has a green head, black back, white sides and chest

Juvenile: same as female

Nest: cavity; female lines an old woodpecker cavity; 1 brood per year

Eggs: 9-11; ivory without markings

Incubation: 28-33 days; female incubates

Fledging: 70-80 days; female feeds young

Migration: non-migrator to partial in Wyoming; moves around to find open water

Food: small fish, aquatic insects

Compare: Hard to confuse with other birds. Look for ragged "hair" on back of a red head, a long, pointed orange bill, white chest and chin.

Stan's Notes: Can be seen on just about any open water during the winter, but more common along large rivers than lakes. This is a shallow water diver that feeds on fish in 10-15 feet (3-4.5 m) of water. The bill has a fine, serrated-like edge to help catch slippery fish. Females often lay their eggs in nests of other mergansers (egg dumping), resulting in broods of up to 15 young per mother. Male leaves the female as soon as she starts to incubate eggs. Orphans are accepted by other merganser mothers with young. Flies back and forth between large rivers and lakes, so check Fishing Bridge and Pelican Bridge in Yellowstone.

in flight

breeding

juvenile

winter

Ring-billed Gull
Larus delawarensis

SUMMER

Size: 19" (48 cm); up to 4-foot wingspan

Male: A white bird with gray wings, black wing tips spotted with white, and a white tail, as seen in flight. Yellow bill with a black ring near the tip. Yellowish legs and feet. Winter or non-breeding adult has a speckled brown back of head and nape of neck.

Female: same as male

Juvenile: brown speckles, a mostly dark bill, brown tip of tail

Nest: ground; female and male construct; 1 brood per year

Eggs: 2-4; off-white with brown markings

Incubation: 20-21 days; female and male incubate

Fledging: 20-40 days; female and male feed young

Migration: complete, to southwestern states and Mexico

Food: insects, fish; scavenges for food

Compare: Franklin's Gull (pg. 259) has a black head. Look for a large white gull with a black ring around the bill near the tip to help identify the Ring-billed Gull.

Stan's Notes: A common gull of garbage dumps and parking lots. This bird is expanding its range and remaining farther north longer during winter due to successful scavenging in cities. A three-year gull with different plumages in its first three fall seasons. Attains the ring on bill after its first winter and adult plumage in the third year. Defends a small area around nest, usually a few feet. Look in large lakes, such as Yellowstone and Jackson Lakes, for this gull.

white morph

blue morph

juvenile

Ross's Goose

in flight

Snow Goose
Anser caerulescens

MIGRATION

Size: 25-38" (63-96 cm); up to 4½-foot wingspan

Male: A mostly white goose with varying patches of black and brown. Black wing tips. Pink bill and legs. Some individuals are grayish with a white head.

Female: same as male

Juvenile: overall dull gray with a dark bill

Nest: ground; female builds; 1 brood per year

Eggs: 3-5; white without markings

Incubation: 23-25 days; female incubates

Fledging: 45-49 days; female and male teach the young to feed

Migration: complete, to southwestern states and Mexico

Food: aquatic insects and plants

Compare: The Trumpeter Swan (pg. 311) is much larger and lacks black wing tips. American White Pelican (pg. 313) shares the black wing tips, but it has a huge bill. Canada Goose (pg. 269) has a black head with a white cheek strap.

Stan's Notes: This bird has two color morphs. The more common white morph is pure white with black wing tips. The gray morph, often called blue, has a white head, gray chest and back, and pink bill and legs. Its thick, serrated bill helps to pull up plants. Breeds in large colonies on the northern Canadian tundra. Females begin breeding at 2-3 years. Older females produce more eggs and are more successful than younger females. Not a resident of Wyoming but seen by the thousands during migration. Very similar to Ross's Goose (see inset), which is slightly smaller with a much smaller pink bill. Often seen with Ross's Geese and Sandhill Cranes.

in flight

juvenile

Trumpeter Swan
Cygnus buccinator

YEAR-ROUND
MIGRATION
WINTER

Size: 60" (152 cm); up to 6½-foot wingspan

Male: A large all-white swan with an all-black bill, legs and feet.

Female: same as male

Juvenile: same size as adult, gray plumage, pinkish gray bill

Nest: ground; female and male construct; 1 brood per year

Eggs: 4-6; creamy white without markings

Incubation: 33-37 days; female incubates

Fledging: 100-120 days; female and male feed young

Migration: partial to non-migrator; moves around to find open water and food

Food: aquatic plants, insects

Compare: Snow Goose (pg. 309) is much smaller than the Trumpeter Swan and has black wing tips.

Stan's Notes: Once hunted to near extinction. Was reintroduced with great success in many parts of its former range; most of the breeding programs were started with eggs taken from Alaskan swans. Often seen with large colored neck or wing tags, which identify the reintroduced individuals. Holds neck with a slight bend or kink at the base. Pairs defend large territories and build large mound nests at the edge of water. Common name comes from its trumpet-like call. If you are seeing a swan in either park, it's a Trumpeter. A year-round resident in the parks, often seen on larger rivers.

breeding

in flight

chick-feeding adult

American White Pelican
Pelecanus erythrorhynchos

MIGRATION
SUMMER

Size: 62" (158 cm); up to 9-foot wingspan

Male: Large white bird with black wing tips that extend partially down the trailing edge of the wings. A white or pale yellow crown. Bright yellow bill, legs and feet. Breeding adult has a bright orange bill and legs. An adult that is feeding chicks (chick-feeding adult) has a gray-black crown.

Female: same as male

Juvenile: duller white with a brownish head and neck

Nest: ground, scraped-out depression rimmed with dirt; female and male build; 1 brood per year

Eggs: 1-3; white without markings

Incubation: 29-36 days; male and female incubate

Fledging: 60-70 days; female and male feed young

Migration: complete, to southwestern states

Food: fish

Compare: Snow Goose (pg. 309) is much smaller and lacks the Pelican's enormous bill.

Stan's Notes: Often in large groups on larger lakes, slow-moving rivers and reservoirs in the state during migration and summer. They feed by simultaneously dipping their bills into the water to scoop up fish; they don't dive into water to catch fish, like coastal Brown Pelicans. Bills and legs of breeding adults turn deep orange. Breeding adults usually also grow a flat, fibrous plate on the upper mandible; this drops off after the eggs hatch. They fly in a large V, often gliding with long wings, then all flapping together. Check any large body of water in both parks, especially Yellowstone Lake and the larger sections of Yellowstone River.

female

Wilson's Warbler
Cardellina pusilla

MIGRATION
SUMMER

Size: 4¾" (12 cm)

Male: Dull yellow upper and bright yellow lower. Distinctive black cap. Large black eyes and small thin bill.

Female: same as male, but lacking the black cap

Juvenile: similar to female

Nest: cup; female builds; 1 brood per year

Eggs: 4-6; white with brown markings

Incubation: 10-13 days; female incubates

Fledging: 8-11 days; female and male feed young

Migration: complete, to coastal Texas, Mexico and Central America

Food: insects

Compare: Orange-crowned Warbler (pg. 323) is paler yellow and lacks the black cap of the male Wilson's Warbler. Male American Goldfinch (pg. 317) has a black forehead and black wings. Male Common Yellowthroat (pg. 319) has a very distinctive black mask.

Stan's Notes: A warbler of mid-level elevations. Can be seen near water in willow and alder thickets. Its all-insect diet makes it one of the top insect-eating birds in North America. Often flicks its tail and spreads its wings when hopping among thick shrubs, looking for insects. The females often mate with males that have the best territories and that might already have mates (polygyny).

winter male

male

female

American Goldfinch
Spinus tristis

YEAR-ROUND

Size: 5" (13 cm)

Male: Perky yellow bird with a black patch on the forehead. Black tail and a conspicuous white rump. Black wings with white wing bars. No marking on the breast. A dramatic change in color during winter, similar to female.

Female: dull olive yellow with brown wings and white rump, lacks a black forehead

Juvenile: same as female

Nest: cup; female builds; 1 brood per year

Eggs: 4-6; pale blue without markings

Incubation: 10-12 days; female incubates

Fledging: 11-17 days; female and male feed young

Migration: partial migrator; small flocks of up to 20 birds move around North America

Food: seeds, insects; will come to seed feeders

Compare: The male Yellow Warbler (pg. 325) is yellow with orange streaks on the chest. Pine Siskin (pg. 103) has a streaked chest and belly and yellow wing bars. The female House Finch (pg. 105) has a heavily streaked chest.

Stan's Notes: A common backyard resident year-round, moving around to find adequate supplies of food during winter. Most often in open fields, scrubby areas and woodlands. Enjoys Nyjer seed in feeders. Breeds in late summer, using the silky down from wild thistle for its nest. Appears roller-coaster-like in flight. Listen for it to twitter during flight. Almost always in small flocks. Often called Wild Canary.

male

female

Common Yellowthroat
Geothlypis trichas

SUMMER

Size: 5" (13 cm)

Male: Olive brown bird with a bright yellow throat and breast, white belly and distinctive black mask outlined in white. A long, thin, pointed black bill.

Female: similar to male, lacks the black mask

Juvenile: same as female

Nest: cup; female builds; 2 broods per year

Eggs: 3-5; white with brown markings

Incubation: 11-12 days; female incubates

Fledging: 10-11 days; female and male feed young

Migration: complete, to southwestern states, Mexico and Central America

Food: insects

Compare: Found in a similar habitat as the American Goldfinch (pg. 317), but lacks the male's black forehead and wings. Yellow-rumped Warbler (pg. 231) has just spots of yellow. The male Yellow Warbler (pg. 325) has fine orange streaks on its chest; both male Yellow Warbler and male Wilson's Warbler (pg. 315) lack the black mask of male Yellowthroat.

Stan's Notes: A common and widespread warbler of open fields and marshes. Song is a cheerful, well-known "witchity-witchity-witchity-witchity," sung from deep within tall grasses. Nests low to the ground in a simple cup nest. The male performs a curious courtship display, bouncing in and out of tall grass while uttering an unusual song. Young remain dependent on their parents longer than most other warblers. A frequent cowbird host.

male
pg. 291

female

American Redstart
Setophaga ruticilla

MIGRATION
SUMMER

Size: 5" (13 cm)

Female: Olive brown with yellow patches on sides, wings and tail. White belly.

Male: small, striking black bird with contrasting patches of orange on sides, wings and tail, white belly

Juvenile: same as female, juvenile male attains orange tinges in the second year

Nest: cup; female builds; 1 brood per year

Eggs: 3-5; off-white with brown markings

Incubation: 12 days; female incubates

Fledging: 9 days; female and male feed young

Migration: complete, to Mexico, Central America and South America

Food: insects, seeds, berries rarely

Compare: Similar to the female Yellow-rumped Warbler (pg. 231), but lacks a yellow patch on rump.

Stan's Notes: A common and widespread warbler throughout Wyoming during migration and summer. Prefers large, unbroken tracts of forest. Appears to be hyperactive when feeding, hovering and darting back and forth to glean insects from leaves. Often droops its wings and fans tail just before launching out to catch an insect. Look for the male's flashing black and orange colors high up in trees.

Orange-crowned Warbler
Leiothlypis celata

MIGRATION
SUMMER

Size: 5" (13 cm)

Male: An overall pale yellow bird with a dark line through eyes. Faint streaking on sides and chest. Small thin bill. Tawny orange crown, often invisible.

Female: same as male, but very slightly duller, often indistinguishable in the field

Juvenile: same as adults

Nest: cup; female builds; 1-2 broods per year

Eggs: 3-6; white with brown markings

Incubation: 12-14 days; female incubates

Fledging: 8-10 days; female and male feed young

Migration: complete, to southwestern states, Mexico and Central America

Food: insects, fruit, nectar

Compare: Male Common Yellowthroat (pg. 319) has a distinctive black mask. Male Wilson's Warbler (pg. 315) is brighter yellow with a distinctive black cap. Yellow Warbler (pg. 325) is darker yellow than the pale yellow of the Orange-crowned Warbler.

Stan's Notes: A nesting resident in Wyoming but often seen more during migration, when large groups move together. Constructs a bulky, well-concealed nest on the ground with nest rim at ground level. Known to drink flower nectar. The orange crown tends to be hidden and is rarely seen in the field. A widespread breeder, from Alaska to across Canada, Montana, Wyoming and beyond.

male

female

Yellow Warbler
Setophaga petechia

MIGRATION
SUMMER

Size: 5" (13 cm)

Male: Yellow warbler with orange streaks on the chest and belly. Long, pointed dark bill.

Female: same as male, but lacks orange streaking

Juvenile: similar to female, only much duller

Nest: cup; female builds; 1 brood per year

Eggs: 4-5; white with brown markings

Incubation: 11-12 days; female incubates

Fledging: 10-12 days; female and male feed young

Migration: complete, to southwestern states, Mexico, Central and South America

Food: insects

Compare: Yellow-rumped Warbler (pg. 231) has just spots of yellow unlike the orange streaks on the yellow chest of male Yellow Warbler. Male American Goldfinch (pg. 317) has a black forehead and wings. Female Yellow Warbler is similar to the female American Goldfinch (pg. 317), but it lacks white wing bars.

Stan's Notes: Widespread and common in parts of Wyoming, seen in gardens and shrubby areas near water. A prolific insect eater, gleaning small caterpillars and other insects from tree leaves. Male is usually seen higher up in trees than the female. Female is less conspicuous. Starts migrating south in August; returns in late April. Males arrive 1-2 weeks before the females to claim territory. Migrates during the night in mixed flocks of warblers. Rests and feeds during the day. Check woodlands around Fishing Bridge Museum. Any wet meadow in Hayden Valley is another good spot.

male
pg. 299

female

Red Crossbill
Loxia curvirostra

YEAR-ROUND

Size: 6½" (16 cm)

Female: A pale yellow-gray sparrow-sized bird with a pale yellow chest and light gray patch on the throat. Dark brown wings. Short dark brown tail. Long, pointed crossed bill.

Male: dirty red to orange with a bright red crown and rump, dark brown wings, a short dark brown tail and a crossed bill

Juvenile: streaked with tinges of yellow, bill gradually crosses about 2 weeks after fledging

Nest: cup; female builds; 1 brood per year

Eggs: 3-4; bluish white with brown markings

Incubation: 14-18 days; female incubates

Fledging: 16-20 days; female and male feed young

Migration: non-migrator to irruptive; moves around the state in winter to find food; will wander as far south as Mexico

Food: seeds, leaf buds; comes to seed feeders

Compare: Larger than the female American Goldfinch (pg. 317). Look for the unique crossed bill.

Stan's Notes: The long crossed bill is adapted for extracting seeds from pine and spruce cones, its favorite food. Often dangles upside down like a parrot to reach cones. Also seen on the ground where it eats grit, which helps digest food. Nests in coniferous forests. Some studies show up to nine distinct populations of Red Crossbills, but they are nearly impossible to distinguish in the field. Plumage can be highly variable among individuals. Irruptive behavior makes it more common in some winters and nonexistent in others.

female

male
pg. 23

Bobolink
Dolichonyx oryzivorus

MIGRATION
SUMMER

Size: 7" (18 cm)

Female: Pale yellow bird with dark brown stripes on the head. Thin dark line extends through the eye. Dark streaks on back and sides.

Male: nearly all-black bird with pale yellow on back of head and nape of neck, white patch on wings and rump

Juvenile: similar to female, lacking dark streaks

Nest: ground; scraped-out depression lined with grass; 1 brood per year

Eggs: 4-6; gray to red brown with brown markings

Incubation: 10-13 days; female incubates

Fledging: 10-14 days; female and male feed young

Migration: complete, to South America, mostly Brazil

Food: insects, seeds

Compare: Smaller than Western Meadowlark (pg. 339) and lacks the obvious black V marking on its breast. Smaller and more yellow than the female Red-winged Blackbird (pg. 141), with dark brown stripes on its head.

Stan's Notes: A member of the blackbird family. Closely related to meadowlarks. A common bird of prairies, grasslands and open fields. In spring, the male will perch on plant stems and repeat its bubbling "bob-o-link" song (which provided the common name). Gives a loud, repeated "ink" whistle during flight. When disturbed, the female will run from her highly concealed ground nest before taking flight. By late summer, the males will have molted to a drab color similar to the females.

male

non-breeding male

female

Western Tanager
Piranga ludoviciana

SUMMER

Size: 7½" (18.5 cm)

Male: A canary yellow bird with a red head. Black back, tail, wings. One white and one yellow wing bar. Non-breeding lacks the red head.

Female: duller than male, lacking the red head

Juvenile: similar to female

Nest: cup; female builds; 1 brood per year

Eggs: 3-5; light blue with brown markings

Incubation: 11-13 days; female incubates

Fledging: 13-15 days; female and male feed young

Migration: complete, to Mexico and Central America

Food: insects, fruit

Compare: The unique coloring makes the breeding male Tanager easy to identify. American Goldfinch (pg. 317) male has a black forehead. Female Bullock's Oriole (pg. 333) lacks the female Tanager's single yellow wing bars.

Stan's Notes: The male Western has stunning breeding plumage. Feeds mainly on insects, such as bees, wasps, cicadas and grasshoppers, and to a lesser degree on fruit. The male feeds the female while she incubates. Female builds a cup nest in a horizontal fork of a coniferous tree, well away from the main trunk, 20-40 feet (6-12 m) aboveground. This is the farthest nesting tanager species, reaching far up into the Northwest Territories of Canada. An early fall migrant, often seen migrating in late July (when non-breeding males lack red heads). Seen in many habitats during migration. Check the conifers on the road to Bunsen Peak. The Tower Fall and Canyon areas are also good places to look.

male pg. 293

female

Bullock's Oriole
Icterus bullockii

SUMMER

Size: 8" (20 cm)

Female: Dull yellow head and breast. Gray-to-black wings with white wing bars. Pale white belly. Gray back, as seen in flight.

Male: bright orange and black with a bold white patch on the wings

Juvenile: similar to female

Nest: pendulous; female and male build; 1 brood per year

Eggs: 4-6; pale white to gray with brown markings

Incubation: 12-14 days; female incubates

Fledging: 12-14 days; female and male feed young

Migration: complete, to Central and South America

Food: insects, berries, nectar; visits nectar feeders

Compare: Female Western Tanager (pg. 331) has a black back unlike female Oriole's gray back. Look for the overall dull yellow and gray appearance of the female Bullock's Oriole.

Stan's Notes: So closely related to Baltimore Orioles of the eastern U.S., at one time both were considered one species. Interbreeds with Baltimores where ranges overlap. Most common in Wyoming where cottonwood trees grow along rivers and other wetlands. Also seen at the edge of clearings, in city parks, on farms and along irrigation ditches. Builds a hanging sock-like nest with plant fibers such as the inner bark of junipers and willows. Will incorporate yarn and thread into the nest if offered during nest building.

male

juvenile

female

Evening Grosbeak

Coccothraustes vespertinus

YEAR-ROUND
WINTER

Size: 8" (20 cm)

Male: A striking bird with a stocky body, a large ivory-to-greenish bill and bright yellow eyebrows. Dirty yellow head, yellow rump and belly and black-and-white wings and tail.

Female: similar to male, with softer colors and a gray head and throat

Juvenile: similar to female, with a brown bill

Nest: cup; female builds; 1 brood per year

Eggs: 3-4; blue with brown markings

Incubation: 12-14 days; female incubates

Fledging: 13-14 days; female and male feed young

Migration: irruptive; moves around Wyoming in winter in search of food

Food: seeds, insects, fruit; comes to seed feeders

Compare: Larger than its close relative, the American Goldfinch (pg. 317). Look for the dark head, bright yellow eyebrows and large thick bill to identify the male Evening Grosbeak.

Stan's Notes: One of the largest finches. Characteristic undulating finch-like flight. An unusually large bill for cracking seeds, its main food source. Often seen on gravel roads eating gravel, from which it gets minerals, salt and grit to grind the seeds it eats. Sheds the outer layer of its bill in spring, exposing a blue green bill. Moves in flocks during winter, searching for food and coming to feeders. More numerous in some years than others; sometimes completely absent. Over the past 30-50 years populations have plummeted. Once very common at feeders in winter, now very uncommon.

Western Kingbird
Tyrannus verticalis

SUMMER

Size: 9" (22.5 cm)

Male: Bright yellow belly and yellow under wings. Gray head and chest, often with a white chin. Wings and tail are dark gray to nearly black with white outer edges on the tail.

Female: same as male

Juvenile: similar to adult, less yellow and more gray

Nest: cup; female and male build; 1 brood per year

Eggs: 3-4; white with brown markings

Incubation: 18-20 days; female incubates

Fledging: 16-18 days; female and male feed young

Migration: complete, to Central America

Food: insects, berries

Compare: Eastern Kingbird (pg. 237) lacks the yellow of Western Kingbird. Western Meadowlark (pg. 339) shares the yellow belly of Western Kingbird, but Meadowlark has a distinctive V-shaped black necklace.

Stan's Notes: A bird of open country, often seen sitting on top of the same shrub or fence post. Hunts by watching for crickets, bees, grasshoppers and other insects and flying out to catch them, then returns to perch. Parents teach young how to hunt, bringing wounded insects back to the nest for the young to chase. Returns in March to April. Builds nest right away, often in the fork of a small single trunk tree. Common throughout Wyoming, nesting in trees around homesteads and farms.

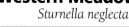

Western Meadowlark
Sturnella neglecta

YEAR-ROUND
SUMMER

Size: 9" (22.5 cm)

Male: Heavy-bodied bird with a short tail. Yellow chest, brown back, and prominent V-shaped black necklace. White outer tail feathers.

Female: same as male

Juvenile: same as adult

Nest: cup, on the ground in dense cover; female builds; 2 broods per year

Eggs: 3-5; white with brown markings

Incubation: 13-15 days; female incubates

Fledging: 11-13 days; female and male feed young

Migration: partial migrator to non-migrator; moves far enough south to escape winter and find food

Food: insects, seeds

Compare: Western Kingbird (pg. 337) shares the yellow belly, but lacks the V-shaped black necklace Horned Lark (pg. 129) lacks the yellow chest and belly. Look for a black V marking on the chest to help identify Western Meadowlark.

Stan's Notes: A bird of open grassy country. Named "Meadowlark" because it's a bird of meadows and sings like the larks of Europe. Best known for its wonderful song–a flute-like, clear whistle. Often seen perching on fence posts but quickly dives into tall grass when approached. Conspicuous white marks on sides of tail, seen when flying away. Nest is sometimes domed with dried grass. Not in the lark family; a blackbird family member and is related to grackles and orioles. Overall population is down greatly due to agricultural activities and ditch mowing. Look in Gros Ventre Campground in the Tetons and Lamar Valley in Yellowstone.

HELPFUL RESOURCES

Wyoming Hotlines

To report unusual bird sightings or possibly hear recordings of where birds have been seen, you can often call pre-recorded hotlines detailing such information. Since these hotlines are usually staffed by volunteers, and phone numbers and even the organizations that host them often change, the phone numbers are not listed here. To obtain the numbers, go to your favorite internet search engine, type in something like "rare bird alert hotline Wyoming" or "rare bird alert Yellowstone" and follow the links provided.

Web Pages

The internet is a valuable place to learn more about birds. You may find birding on the net a fun way to discover additional information or to spend a long winter night. These websites will assist you in your pursuit of birds. If a web address doesn't work (they often change a bit), just enter the name of the group into a search engine to track down the new web address.

Site	Address
Audubon Rockies Wyoming Chapters	rockies.audubon.org/chapters/ wyoming-chapters
Yellowstone Valley Audubon Society	www.yvaudubon.org
American Birding Association	www.aba.org
Cornell Lab of Ornithology	www.birds.cornell.edu
Author Stan Tekiela's home page	www.naturesmart.com

CHECKLIST/INDEX BY SPECIES

Use the boxes to check the birds you've seen.

MORE FOR THE NORTHWEST BY STAN TEKIELA

Bird Identification Guides
Birds of Idaho Field Guide
Birds of Montana Field Guide
Birds of Oregon Field Guide
Birds of Washington Field Guide
Birds of Prey of the West
  Field Guide

Backyard Bird Feeding Guides
Bluebirds
Cardinals
Finches
Hummingbirds
Orioles
Woodpeckers

Wildlife Photography Puzzles
Goldfinch in the Garden
Gray Wolf Eyes
Moose at the Mountains
Red-bellied Woodpecker

Children's Books
Baby Bear Discovers the World
C is for Cardinal
Critter Litter
The Cutest Critter
Do Beavers Need Blankets?
Jump, Little Wood Ducks
Some Babies Are Wild
Super Animal Powers
Whose Butt?

Adventure Quick Guides
Birds of the Northwest

Nature's Wild Cards
Birds of the Northwest
  Playing Cards
Mammals of the Northwest
  Playing Cards
Trees of the Northwest
  Playing Cards
Hummingbirds Playing Cards

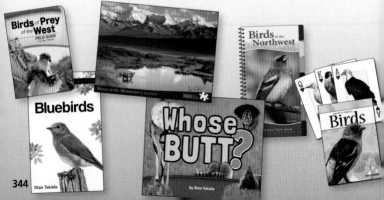

ABOUT THE AUTHOR

Naturalist, wildlife photographer and writer Stan Tekiela is the originator of the popular state-specific field guide series that includes *Birds of Montana Field Guide*. Stan has authored more than 190 educational books, including field guides, quick guides, nature books, children's books, playing cards and more, presenting many species of animals and plants.

With a Bachelor of Science degree in Natural History from the University of Minnesota and as an active professional naturalist for more than 30 years, Stan studies and photographs wildlife throughout the United States and Canada. He has received various national and regional awards for his books and photographs. Also a well-known columnist and radio personality, his syndicated column appears in more than 25 newspapers, and his wildlife programs are broadcast on a number of Midwest radio stations. Stan can be followed on Facebook and Twitter. He can be contacted via www.naturesmart.com.